I'm Dying to Tell You

PRAISE FOR NEIL HOOD'S BOOKS

God's Payroll: Whose work is it anyway?

"Professor Hood had a huge appetite for work which was matched by his commitment to his faith. He personified the values he espoused in *God's Payroll*. The book itself is well researched and is, where appropriate, scholarly, but it is above all a practical guide for those of us who are concerned about our capacity to infuse our working life with Christian values. This is a fine book and deserves to be widely read."
Robert Crawford, Chief Executive, Scottish Enterprise Network

"Throughout his life, Neil Hood consistently interwove his faith within the pattern of his business and personal life. The characteristic of his profile was a dominant feature in all serious contributions he made in commerce, industry, education and within the Christian Church."
Donald McDonald, McDonald Hotels

"Work and faith are only too readily separated. Neil challenged that basis for Christian living, and did so powerfully and biblically. You might not find it comfortable, but we all need to read this and take it to heart."
Sir Peter Vardy, Chief Executive, Reg Vardy plc

"I believe that those who read this book, follow its advice, and accept its challenges, will find that their view of work will conform more closely with the other central aspects of their Christian life as they learn to glorify God and enjoy Him forever."
Lord Mackay of Clashfern, former Lord Chancellor

"A must-have for all those striving to seek the relevance of their faith in contemporary culture."
Steve Chalke, Oasis Global

"A compelling, practical and insightful guide."
Stephen Gaukroger

"A comprehensive guide to the peaks and troughs of the workplace which is highly recommended."
Dr Steve Brady, Principal, Moorlands College

"A book that will encourage and empower Christians in their working lives. In a field that pastors and church leaders have unjustly neglected, *God's Payroll* is just what we need!"
Julian Hardyman, Eden Baptist Church, Cambridge

God's Wealth: Whose money is it anyway?

"When an assiduous Bible student like Neil Hood is able to apply his deep understanding of the scriptures to his life in business the result is a book of tremendous value to modern Christians."
Richard Bewes, former Rector, All Souls, Langham Place, London

"What is more interesting than money? I would encourage everyone to read this simple, thoughtful book and find out. It could change your life!"
Professor Ewan Brown CBE, Chairman, Lloyds TSB Scotland plc

"We live in a material world in which money is an essential part of our lives. This book challenges us to think outside the box in which we live and to think about what God intended our resources to be used for."
Andrew Buxton, former chairman of Barclays Bank plc

"Mega relevant, hyper refreshing, cutting edge, out of the box yet biblical!"
George Verwer, Founder, Operation Mobilisation

"A thoughtful contribution to a much neglected topic – the nature of Christian teaching on finance."
Rt Hon Paul Boateng MP, Chief Secretary to the Treasury

"I love Neil's writing. It's thoroughly biblical and provokingly practical. I also knew the man and that makes his writings even more challenging for me."
Peter Maiden

Whose life is it anyway?

"Neil was a gutsy compassionate guy who mysteriously fused academia, business acumen and commonsense into one personality. His Christian lifestyle and ethos made him equally relaxed talking to steelworkers and captains of industry alike."
Brian Soutar, Chairman, Stagecoach Holdings plc

"Neil Hood drew on his huge professional portfolio and experience as a Bible teacher to equip us as effective disciples and good stewards of our time and resources. Whoever you are and whatever you do, effective Christian lifestyle comes within easy reach."
Rev Joel Edwards, General Director, Evangelical Alliance UK

"At some point or another, you're going to ask yourself the question that Neil Hood asked in his immensely helpful book . . . With realism and practicality he guided us through the blessings of the biblical answer, and with the concern and encouragement of a fellow-traveller he urged us to keep choosing to live to Christ. In a self-serving world, we need a book like this."
Dominic Smart

"A meticulous and thought-provoking book written from a wealth of experience."
Rob Parsons

"Neil's writings will be of great interest to a wide spectrum of people and will make many stop, think and hopefully adopt those 'pointers' that will help us all improve our approach to life."
Sir Tom Farmer, Founder, Kwik-Fit Holdings plc

"Over the last 10 years Neil Hood consistently gave me excellent and well balanced advice and I am sure his reliability is based on the Christian faith. Running a business which depends on partnering with large organisations, I can't stress too much the importance of trust in modern business relationships. What Neil both preached and practised goes to the heart of these principles."
Hilary Cropper CBE, Execuive Chairman, Xansa plc

"Neil had a set of values and interests which are second to none. His wide ranging and far reaching business interests combined seamlessly with his Christian beliefs and his academic life. How he got the time to write a book, I'll never know!"
Sir Ian Robinson, Chairman, Hilton Group plc

I'm Dying to Tell You

Neil Hood

Authentic

Copyright © 2006 Neil Hood

12 11 10 09 08 07 06   7 6 5 4 3 2 1

First published 2006 by Authentic Media, 9 Holdom Avenue, Bletchley, Milton Keynes, Bucks MK1 1QR, UK and 285 Lynnwood Avenue, Tyrone, GA 30290, USA OM Authentic Media Medchal Road, Jeedimetla Village, Secunderabad 500 055, A.P.

www.authenticmedia.co.uk

Authentic Media is a division of Send the Light Ltd., a company limited by guarantee (registered charity no. 270162)

British Library Cataloguing in Publication Data

A catalogue record for this book is available from the British Library

ISBN-13 978-1-85078-680-1

ISBN-10 1-85078-680-1

Cover design by fourninezero design. Design and Typesetting by Temple Design, Manchester Printed in Great Britain by J.H. Haynes & Co. Ltd., Sparkford

To the glory of God who guides seekers to Jesus Christ; and in profound gratitude to the global army of prayer warriors who have sustained Anna and me and our family (Annette, Alan and Emily; Cameron, Ann, Isla and Sarah) during my illness. Once more, without your support and the Spirit's leading, this book would never have been written.

Neil Hood, CBE, DBA, FRSE (1943-2006), juggled a busy life as an international business strategist, university professor, company director, Christian conference speaker, prolific author on international business and economic development, family man and church elder. He was Emeritus Professor of Business Policy at the University of Strathclyde, Glasgow, UK, and a director of, or advisor to, a number of major companies. He had been a non-executive director of eight public companies, including Reg Vardy plc and British Polythene Industries plc. He had advised many governments and international agencies on economic matters. He was Chairman of Scottish Equity Partners Ltd and former Deputy Chairman of Scottish Enterprise. In 2000 he was honoured by Queen Elizabeth for services to business and economic development. His life plan to dedicate his time and skills to Christian ministries was reflected in his being appointed President of Send the Light Limited in 2005, in his involvement with Christian ministries such as Blythswood Care and International Christian College, and in his busy preaching and teaching schedule. He and his wife, Anna, had two children, Annette (married to Alan) and Cameron (married to Ann), and three grandchildren, Emily, Isla and Sarah. Neil was not too busy, however, to grow orchids, cheer on the Scottish rugby team and play with his grandchildren.

Contents

Preface 13
Introduction 17
Acknowledgements 19

I Stumbling Blocks **21**

1. Where am I? 23
   Where did you come from, and how did you get here? 24
   Where I'm coming from *31*
   Stumbling blocks *33*

2. Where is God? 43
   Introduction *44*
   Three biblical love stories *45*
   Stumbling blocks *53*

3. How will we meet? 66
   Making the connection *67*
   Stages of the journey *69*
   Life stories *73*
   Stumbling block *81*

II Stepping Stones **85**

4. What's missing in my life? 87
   Do voids exist? *88*
   What's missing? *89*
   From stumbling blocks to stepping stones *100*

5. What's on offer? 106
   What does it look like? *107*
   What's in it for me? *115*
   Defer, reject, negotiate, accept *119*

6. What's the journey like? 123
  Introduction 124
  Tests of faith 128
  Doubts 130
  Life stories 131

III New Foundations 141

7. How do I become a Christian? 143
  New foundations 144
  Glimpses of God 147
  Steps on the way to Jesus 148
  Paul 152
  Life stories 154

8. How do I choose? 163
  Decisions, decisions 164
  Developing a relationship with Jesus 166
  Why Jesus? 168
  Stumbling blocks – Heaven and hell 175

9. Can I handle the consequences? 182
  Actions and reactions 183
  Breaking the cycle 185
  Handling the consequences in real life 187

10. What happens now? 199
  Where were you? 200
  What happens now? 201
  What did they do? 207

Preface

Neil Hood was a remarkable man.

Those of you who were not privileged to know him personally probably knew of him and his many and varied achievements. His success in academia demonstrated his intellectual calibre; the roles he attained in business spoke volumes about his wisdom and judgement; his contributions in public service confirmed his interest in bettering the lot of his compatriots or, as Jesus would have put it, his neighbours.

Neil succeeded in whatever he did. His glittering career was not achieved at the expense of his family. There was no better husband, no more adored father and no more adoring grandfather than he was! Few gained more friends than Neil did. The friends of his youth stayed friends for life and were added to, rather than replaced by, a host of others. No one could have attracted and held the affection of so many from such a spectrum of ages, backgrounds, interests, abilities and personalities were they not, as Neil was, specially gifted in and committed to friendship.

In his youth, Neil became a disciple of Jesus and never once did this commitment waver. His faith shaped his character and determined his actions. It also brought another area of success, which was Neil's church life. He was in demand as a gifted preacher and was involved in international organizations and charities. But the mainstay of his church life was the local evangelical church in which he served for almost forty years, providing leadership throughout most of these years. The many acts of kindness from members of that church, which were given unobtrusively throughout Neil's long illness, are silent witnesses to the place he had won in their hearts.

The award of the CBE showed that Neil's qualities had been noticed in high places. His long illness suggests that his faith and obedience were discussed in even higher places. A few thousand years ago, God and Satan discussed the success of another remarkable man. "What do you make of Job?" asked God. "There's nobody like him; he's blameless and upright." "Are you surprised?" responded Satan. "He doesn't do it for nothing. Look at the way he's prospered. Change his circumstances, and he will curse you to your face!" Perhaps a similar conversation took place a few short years ago and God allowed Satan to put our remarkable man to the test.

Throughout the first phase of his illness Neil continued working and serving in a way that won respect for his courage and determination. As a result he received comments of admiration and was able to engage people in conversations about what *really* matters – which were a source of encouragement to him. Because of his physical state, however, he was not able to live the long months of the latter stage of his illness in public. A very public man was deprived of the multiple companionships that had marked his life, and it was in this relative isolation that he attained his greatest achievement. He accepted and proved God's promise, "My grace is sufficient for you, for my power is made perfect in weakness" (2 Corinthians 12:9).

In his book *Learning at the Crossroads* Neil made the bold statement, "I have total assurance that . . . what the Lord intends me to do will not be left undone", and in the final stage of his illness he concentrated his failing physical and mental resources on doing what God wanted. He did so by encouraging others, praying for others and writing this book. In doing so, he placed himself among that small band of dying men and women for whom self becomes less and less important. Some of us know the benefits of the encouragements he gave. In eternity, many will discover the importance of the prayers he offered for them. Many of you will be challenged by what you read in this, his last book.

In the final weeks of his life he prepared the outline of another book, on "redeeming the time", and started accumulating material that would have been useful in writing it. So this, while it is his final book, is not a dying man's attempt to persuade you to believe something. Neil lived a remarkable life because he shared it with Jesus.

Neil Hood was a remarkable man and he wanted to introduce you to Jesus, the most remarkable Man he had ever met.

Ian Clark, CBE, LL.D
March 2006

Introduction

I have written this book out of my passion to introduce men and women to the joy of faith in Jesus Christ. My greatest desire is that you would know the freedom of forgiveness; that you would understand how Christian principles are worked out in practice; that you would see clearly the difference that Christian faith would make to your life and future. I have met many people over the years with whom I wanted to share a book like this (not necessarily written by me!) that explains the Christian faith. So I have not come quickly or lightly to this task.

For over forty years I have taught the Christian faith in many different contexts, from churches, conferences and conventions; to university, college and school campuses; hotels, conference centres and stadia. But one-on-one conversations are perhaps the most fruitful context for teaching, trying to work out Christian values in the routines of everyday life. My hope is that you will enter into the dialogue here, in reading this book and in follow-up conversations with Christian friends and colleagues. This book addresses crucial but challenging issues that will bring many questions to your mind. Ask these questions! Bring them to Christians you know or to leaders in your local church. Search out the truth until you find it.

I found the truth of Jesus Christ many years ago, and it transformed my life. Hence my passion to write, from my hospital bed, this book you now hold in your hands. Following a recurrence of cancer in early 2005, and whilst undergoing chemotherapy treatment, I broke my femur in an accident in June 2005 and spent over four months in hospital. In spite of painful circumstances, I have found great joy in writing this book and hope that in reading it you, too, will come to know the peace and forgiveness that only Jesus can give.

The book asks ten logical questions, in three sections, bringing you over stumbling blocks to stepping stones and finally to building new foundations. You will find answers to the fundamental questions: What does it mean to be a Christian? Who is Jesus Christ and what did he do? And what does that have to do with me?

Acknowledgements

With this, the fifth Christian book I've written, the list of those deserving acknowledgement has grown ever longer. The feedback from the readers of the *Whose Life . . .* trilogy and *Learning at the Crossroads* has continued to be a great encouragement and blessing to me. I am grateful for the persistent prayers of countless people across the world as I wrote this book from my hospital bed. I also want to thank those who have kindly endorsed the book, several of whom have been long-term supporters. The contributions of the publishing and production team have been as vital as ever. Irene Hood, my personal assistant, continues to be a tower of strength for her support, organizational skills and attention to detail. Mark Finnie and all the Authentic team are, as always, a great source of guidance and encouragement on the publishing and production fronts; and my editor, Tara Smith, is as provocative, clear-thinking and thought-stimulating as ever. She has made a massive contribution to all of these books.

Neil Hood
January 2006

I

Stumbling Blocks

1

Where am I?

"The LORD looks down from heaven on the human race to see if there are any who understand, any who seek God." (Psalm 14:2)

"You will seek me and find me when you seek me with all your heart." (Jeremiah 29:13)

Outline

Where did you come from, and how did you get here? A spiritual GPS to help you plot your location. What are your attitudes toward and experiences of God? What is your style of approaching the Christian faith?

Where I'm coming from: An explanation of my beliefs and assumptions.

Stumbling blocks: Stumbling blocks, or "traps", have always made it difficult for people to find the truth of faith. Two of the most fundamental stumbling blocks to faith are the God of the Bible and the Bible itself.

Where did you come from, and how did you get here?

"You can't get there from here," the old farmer said to the city chap seeking directions. You can, of course, but you do need to know where you are before you can get where you're going. Everybody comes from somewhere. There is an amazing diversity of cultures, family backgrounds, career paths, religious experiences and so on in this world. Individual spiritual awareness is equally diverse. What, for example, caused you to pick up this book? How you read its contents will, in part, reflect your attitudes towards faith in general and your experiences with Christians and their faith in particular.

We all put our faith in something. For some of us, success, recognition and money are proxy "gods". For others of us it may be family, relationships, good causes – any number of good things that in and of themselves will never meet our deepest needs or calm our unspoken fears. Most people today are seeking something that keeps eluding them. Colleagues and friends have asked me why I live my life the way I do and what drives me. Sometimes we can base our dialogue on the common foundation of the Judaeo/Christian tradition – although for most people, residual beliefs based on that tradition are but dusty curiosities from three generations past. But we can have this conversation about faith, you and I, if you come to this book with an open mind and a willingness to consider matters that you may have discounted, criticized or rejected. I know that's not always easy to do – but trust me, it's worth it!

First, then, it's important to take some time out for self-analysis. You will then be able to assess whether your perspective changes as you read through this book and reflect on these issues of faith. Table 1.1 describes seven different attitudes that may help you to identify your own position with reference to the Christian faith. The list is by no means exhaustive. As we will see throughout this book, the world bombards us with messages that discourage us from taking the Christian faith seriously. Nor is it easy to overcome our personal obstacles to faith – pride, fierce independence, priorities and personal goals, self-image, power and so on.

Table 1.1 Past experience

My experience of Christian faith has made me ...	*I agree with some or all of the following:*
Hostile	The church is riddled with hypocrisy and even immorality.
	Church members seem more interested in running social clubs than reaching the needy.
	The church is largely silent or inconsistent when confronted by great matters of national and international concern.
	My experience of forced church attendance has soured me for life.
	I see no way back – not that I'm looking for a way right now anyway.
Indifferent	I know some fine Christians.
	I draw the line at attempts to "convert" me.
	I have yet to hear anything from the Bible that could give me a better life.
	Frankly, I don't care whether or not God exists.

Cynical	How can intelligent people get anything from belief in a global saviour, faith, prayer and so on?
	Church is like a medieval drama enacted by the weak-willed and a paid-up insurance policy for the nervous.
	There is nothing after this life, heaven or hell, and I simply don't buy any of this.
Confused	Growing up, my family regularly attended church. During my teenage years I chose to opt out and drifted into other interests.
	I've done a lot of reading on all types of religions and cults. I'm so much better informed than in my early years, but I'm also very confused.
	I don't know what to believe and I'm swayed for a time by each new well-argued book I find on the web. Frankly, I don't know where I'm coming from!
Untrusting	Although I'm an agnostic, I was determined to allow our children to make their own choices about religious belief. When situations of abuse in local churches came to light, however, we withdrew our children from all church activities.
	I feel like I may have let my children down by not giving them a foundation in a faith. While I know that those were isolated cases of abuse and I cannot believe that if there is a God he or she would permit this to happen, I still cannot bring myself to trust the institution of the church.

Neutral	I'm open to persuasion, but not yet persuaded.
	Rightly or wrongly, my problem is role models. I haven't met many Christians in whose lives I can see that Jesus' teachings have made any direct impact.
	I accept that the leader of the faith can be the only perfect model – but I could use some more effective interpreters around me.
	I'm travelling on a journey and books like this, if they are honest about the struggles and challenges of faith, intrigue me.
A spectator	I love church architecture, music and ceremony. But it's all a bit like entering a time capsule.
	I attend major church events at Christmas and Easter. We even build our family day around them. It's part of who we are as a nation and central to our heritage.
	None of this, however, has anything to do with faith. Rather, it fills a cultural void and gives me a sense of having roots in rapidly changing times.
A member	While church attendance falls sharply, I remain a "member" because it gives me social standing and I can support a local institution and a good minister.
	I rarely attend and could not claim to get value from my subscription. Church is a place for "rites of passage" and not much else.
	Occasionally, I feel mildly embarrassed and even hypocritical about my position.

Reflection:

Where are you in terms of thinking about or reacting to Christianity? How would you summarize how you arrived where you are now (thinking about the influences of key people, your background, experiences and so on)? What is your biggest question regarding the Christian faith?

Let me "introduce" you to a few people who have different perspectives on this whole subject of faith. Do you recognize anything of yourself here?

Martin has no interest in Christianity, but he is sympathetic to my Christian perspective and reads any literature I give him – including books I have written. However, he still sees my commitment as being to a church grouping and refuses to see the need for a personal faith in Jesus which is independent of any given church. This attitude perhaps reflects his upbringing, but it also keeps him in his comfort zone. He thinks he could maintain a relationship with God by occasionally attending a church. As it happens, he never does.

Frank is a senior academic. He is a scientist, but he has a philosopher's interest in faiths. He is widely read, loves debate and is highly articulate. He thrives on controversy. He attends a traditional high church mainly for the music and ceremony, although he appreciates a well-crafted sermon. We have had many heated discussions. He finds my approach to faith too robust, too black and white and altogether too demanding on a believer's lifestyle. He also wants to leave open the possibility that there are many routes to God other than Jesus Christ.

Norman is a sociologist, an atheist and a fully paid-up cynic in all matters relating to the Christian faith. Each Christian he meets is a fresh specimen in his laboratory of life. He tries to predict, for example, what my attitudes will be to news items, world events and so on. In spite of his pride in his own liberal sentiments, he has completely closed his mind to the idea that God could have any influence on his life. His family relationships have been very painful, but he sees no role for God there either. He sets the Bible right up there with nursery rhymes and fairy tales.

Janice follows a sad, but rather common, pattern. Her life has been shattered by of a series of misfortunes in which "God let her down". A devout and devoted couple, Janice and Richard farmed in a beautiful rural setting and were very involved in the local church and community. Their barns frequently resounded with the happy noises of youth groups and camps. They actively practised their faith. Then disaster struck. One evening, Richard was moving a heavy tractor in the yard when he accidentally struck their five-year-old son, Joe. Joe died two days later as a result of complications from major surgery. The family and community were distraught and racked by that most difficult of questions: "Why?" Ten years later, Richard has no faith; Janice struggles on. There are no simple answers to their pain.

Anonymous. I don't know this person's name, because when s/he sent a defaced copy of my first Christian book to my office, he or she chose not to disclose it. I was disappointed, but not completely surprised. God warned his followers that people would oppose them because of their beliefs, and I had published a challenging and hard-hitting book on Christian lifestyle.[1]

As we are beginning to see, people look for God in many different ways. Identifying your approach to the Christian faith in Table 1.2 now will give you a point of reference as you read further.

---

[1] Neil Hood, *Whose Life is it Anyway?* (Carlisle: Authentic Lifestyle, 2002).

Table 1.2 How different people look for God

Type of approach	Characteristics
Focused	Usually near the end of his or her search, often following an external event or a new spiritual experience which heightens an awareness of God.
	Looking for a solution to bring their search to an end.
	Likely to be very aware of the need for forgiveness and driven by a desire for the truth.
	This may be a distressing time but can end in great joy when the search for Jesus is complete and forgiveness experienced.
Casual	Much less well-ordered, his or her search ebbs and flows, sometimes for years.
	Events or conversations may fuel the search at times, but other priorities take precedence and crowd out an interest in faith.
	Some questions are just too difficult to resolve, and the search gets called off regularly.
	God often appears distant and tough to connect with.
Eclectic	Open to any and every new idea about spirituality that feeds the mind.
	Being selective, and placing a high value on flexibility, he or she often finds the demands of Jesus too rigid.

	A "café approach", selecting items off the menu and not committing to anything that makes serious personal demands.
	Usually experiences confusion as a result of the various options collected.
Passive	On stand-by: there will be a time to think of eternal and spiritual matters, but it isn't now.
	This time is rarely specified, but it is usually so far in the future that there is no pressure.
	Few in this group ever actually find God.
Rejecting	Since there is no God to be found, spiritual searches are futile.
	There are plenty of other things in this life worth achieving – success, money, health, etc.
	While bravado may characterize them, there are many discontented people in this group.

Where I'm coming from

Having encouraged you to think through where you are in your faith journey, it is only reasonable to explain my own faith perspective. I am a Christian. My faith in Jesus Christ dates from my teenage years, and I am committed to follow the Bible's teaching by the power of the Holy Spirit. God knows (and I prove daily!) that living the Christian life is impossible without divine help. I have never practised my faith in leafy retreats or among lots of other Christians – quite the contrary! I have worked at the lowest end of the ladder in the steel-making process, spent decades in a university setting with cynical and atheistic academics, and served on many boards with some of the ablest, wealthiest, but least God-fearing people in the land. I have had different roles in public life, working with government ministers for whom the adrenalin of life was power (and, for some of them, "faith" was merely part of the tool kit to get, or maintain, that power). I have encountered some fine Christians in all of these contexts, but relatively few.

It will be impossible to fully explain my Christian beliefs in the context of this book – and, if I were to do so, it would be a dry work of theology. But I will point out my fundamental assumptions at key points throughout the discussion. Among other things, I believe in one sovereign God who rules the world and yet can rule my life by invitation only; I believe that God is unchangeable, and in character simultaneously a God of love, holiness and judgement. I see the all-pervasiveness of sin in our world, and I believe that God forgives our personal sin on the basis of our faith in Jesus Christ and his death on the cross. I believe that God took on human flesh in Jesus Christ and experienced death and resurrection – these are the key events in world history. I believe that, having received forgiveness for our sins through a personal confession of faith, and by the Spirit of God living within us, God offers the Christian a unique and blessed life on earth and eternal life in heaven. Finally, I use the Bible as my textbook because I believe in its claims to contain the word of life. In what follows I set out basic Christian principles in as simple a way as possible, leaving you to make up your own mind about them.

Stumbling blocks

The biblical concept of a "stumbling block" is a simple one. When an animal springs a trap set for it, the trap holds its victim until it is killed or rescued. Many people get "trapped" by a piece of biblical advice or theology that they cannot accept – and they never move on. Throughout this book we will be looking at some of the most common traps with regard to the Christian faith. You will probably recognize many of them. I do you no favour if I avoid telling you what the Bible says on vital issues that affect your future. But, as we shall see in Chapter 8, the choice is always yours.

Stumbling blocks have been around since the time Jesus was on earth, and they have always come in various guises. What causes a problem for one person does not necessarily trap another. If they were not subtle, they would have no power to trap us. Table 1.3 sets out some of the common stumbling blocks and contrasts the form they originally took with their contemporary disguise. The contrasts say much about society today. In New Testament times, the stumbling blocks to faith mainly trapped the Jewish religious authorities, who were arbiters of thinking and guided all other opinions. The issue of "sin", for example, features in both eras, but for quite different reasons. People in Jesus' day saw his claim to forgive sin as blasphemy; to many today it seems totally unnecessary. We will look at the cross in greater detail in Chapter 2. Many at the time regarded it as a disaster and a flimsy foundation for a new faith. Many today think Jesus' death was far too gory and unpleasant – surely salvation could come another way. But it couldn't and it can't. Jesus always spoke without fear or favour. And he still does.

Table 1.3 Stumbling blocks to Christian faith: Then and now

Stumbling block	Perception in New Testament times	Perception in the twenty-first century
Jesus forgives sin	Since only God can forgive sin, Jesus is implying that he is God. This is blasphemy!	Who needs forgiveness these days? I don't "sin" personally, but there is a lot of evil in the world, so God must be to blame for tolerating this.
Jesus socialized with scoundrels	Rabbis shouldn't keep bad company. He should know better.	Jesus was a model of social egalitarianism. We should learn from his example, but we don't need to listen to his message for sinners.
Jesus died on a cross	It was shameful to die on a cross. His death was foolish, premature and unnecessary. What kind of founder of a faith would die like that?	The cross remains a symbol of a dreadful event rather than a display of God's love that is fundamental to his rescue mission (for people who don't see their need to be rescued).
Jesus' teaching is radical and he requires obedience	He demands too much from his followers, turns lives upside down and cuts across accepted social customs and standards.	"Reform" and "lifestyle change" are popular, but being "born again" and giving control of your life to God is going too far.

| Jesus eschews hypocrisy and distorted religion | Why is he picking on the wealthy and those locked in legal religious niceties? | Religion is one thing; challenging my lifestyle, behaviour, possessions and attitudes is quite another. |

Two of the most fundamental stumbling blocks for people thinking about the Christian faith today are God and the Bible.

Stumbling block number 1: The God of the Bible

Most of us, I suspect, have a central philosophical question. Our society puts "religion" and "science" in two separate boxes – the latter does away with the need for the former. Many people will acknowledge that religion is important to others, and they will accept such phrases as "it gives meaning to my life"; and "God is very real to me" as being valid for other people. The debate centres on whether such things are objectively true in the scientific sense. Much of this controversy boils down to the conflict between biblical theism and evolutionary naturalism as articulated by Charles Darwin and many others. This conflict has radically shaped contemporary perspectives on God and has closed many minds to the existence of the God of the Bible, much less to his power in creation or salvation. The eighteenth-century hymn writer Charles Wesley called for a resolution to this debate: "Unite the pair so long disjointed, knowledge and vital piety."

Relatively little has been achieved towards that goal since Wesley's time, however. The products and benefits of "science" are so much more tangible, ubiquitous and evident in this technological age – and it seems an easy matter to ignore God, deciding that he has nothing much to offer. Even more influential, however, are the intellectual intimidation tactics that many influential Darwinists deploy. Richard Dawkins, for example, remarks, "It is absolutely safe to say that if you meet somebody who claims not to believe in evolution, that person is ignorant, stupid or insane." Or again, "The universe we observe has precisely the properties we should expect if there is, at bottom, no design, no purpose, no evil and no good, nothing but blind pitiless existence."[2] In one way or another, this is the kind of hostility and closed-mindedness that Christianity has increasingly faced over the past century.

The faith has not been, and will not be, destroyed by it, but these ideas have been highly influential. Among other things, they have fostered a philosophy of moral equivalence which, in the name of "tolerance", forbids the recognition of any distinction between good and evil. Under the guise of "political correctness", the greatest sins are intolerance and insensitivity. Tragically, generations of intelligent people have subsequently rejected the Christian faith without examining its claims because they assumed it would entail throwing away their mental faculties.

This conflict between religion and science, and how it has shaped our approach to thinking about the Christian faith, is so important that I want to examine one part of it in more detail. I do so because it illustrates what happens when one begins to question the received wisdom on evolution from which so much else flows. The scientific approach is to accept the creation narrative of the Bible as a myth and to acknowledge that the world was formed by a series of natural

---

[2] Richard Dawkins, "Book Review" (of Donald Johanson and Maitland Edey, *Blueprint*), *The New York Times* (9 April 1989), p. 3. See also Phillip E. Johnson, *The Right Questions: Truth, Meaning and Public Debate* (Downers Grove, IL: IVP, 2002), p. 81.

laws in a manner that was random, totally undirected and purposeless. In all of this, there is no scope for God. Christian intellectuals from different disciplines have been challenging these presuppositions in recent years. One of the central strands of this argument is a Bible passage from the Gospel of John chapter 1, verses 1–14. Verse 1 says, "In the beginning was the Word, and the Word was with God, and the Word was God." Phillip Johnson, one of these leaders, writes a parody of this verse from the evolutionist's perspective to draw attention to the fact that all secular learning on this topic is the opposite of this verse and that scientific critics need to address its truth. Here is his parody:

> In the beginning were the particles and the impersonal
> laws of physics,
> And the particles somehow became complex living stuff;
> And the stuff imagined God;
> But then discovered evolution.[3]

You will note that in this dogma there is no "Word", namely no intelligence or purpose. Three things (in addition to chance), therefore, had to do all the creating: first, the particles combined to become "complex living stuff" through a process of evolution, second, that involved only chemical combinations governed by chance and natural law; and, third, rather than God creating humankind, it was the other way around. Having evolved from animals by a mindless natural process, but not having science to tell them what had happened (until Darwin!), primitive humans relied on their own imagination to create God. When we look at it in this way, it seems to me an incredibly flimsy basis for a belief system – let alone one that has been so disruptive and

---

[3] Johnson, *Right Questions*, p. 64.

all-persuasive. I find it impossible to give any credence to the thought that impersonality should somehow produce personality. So I place my faith in the Word of the God of the Bible.

Reflection:

Having looked at the science and theology in great detail, Johnson concludes that "the evidence of science shows that 'in the beginning was the Word' is as true scientifically, as it is true theologically, scripturally and in every other way".[4] What is your view? Has your opinion regarding the biblical view of creation shifted at all? If so, how?

It is important to note that the Bible never tries to prove that God exists. But it is clear that it is God's intention to reveal himself to all of us. Why, then, do so many people have little or no belief in God? These are the same people who recognize the effects of other demanding "gods" such as power, wealth, career and health in their friends and colleagues. Throughout our lives, God has spoken to each one of us. The question is this: Have we listened to him? Broadly speaking, he speaks in two different ways – generally and specifically – but we need help to interpret both. As one author expresses it, "Only God can interpret his own handwriting." This is a vital point and it sounds like a tautology – we need God to open our eyes to see him, our minds to know him and our lips to praise him. For example, God reveals himself to all of us because we are alive and able to marvel at nature, at the beauty of a child, at the colours of a fine garden in bloom, at the wonders of space,

---

[4] Johnson, *Right Questions*, p. 141.

and at the revelations from modern science. The following verse from the Psalms summarizes the Christian understanding: "The heavens declare the glory of God; the skies proclaim the work of his hands."[5] The following verses from the New Testament explain something of the effort that God has made to reach our minds: ". . . since what may be known about God is plain to them, because God has made it plain to them . . . God's invisible qualities – his eternal power and divine nature – have been clearly seen, being understood from what has been made, so that they [human beings] are without excuse".[6] Once you remove the idea of God as the prime mover in the universe, you have done much to destroy faith. Many of us have lost this sense of natural power, order and harmony, and with it one critical building block of the foundation for personal faith.

But what about the more specific disclosures that God makes about himself? Following are just two examples: God as redeemer and as the lord of destiny. The theologian and Bible translator J.B. Phillips spoke about God in dramatic and radical terms, as the inverse of everyday life as we know it. "God is the great reality (not other visible things. The real things of this world are the invisible spiritual realities!). Christianity rests on revelation – we know God because He acted to make Himself known."

First, then, we consider God as redeemer. The Bible begins with the assumption that you and I need to be rescued. Because of the penalty that comes to all humankind from original sin, we need someone to rescue us from slavery

---

[5] Psalm 19:1 (NB: For those unfamiliar with biblical references, these are identified throughout in this format: book of the Bible [here Psalm], followed by the chapter [here 19] and verse [here v. 1]).

[6] Romans 1:19–20.

to sin. That's God's plan implemented through Jesus Christ. "What slavery? And what *sin*?" you retort indignantly. Many people cannot see, accept or believe that they have sinned. The concept implies failure – that things are not quite going right with our lives. That's why it's really difficult to bring this basic truth to the attention of people like you and me. While we have no problem seeing the urgent need for a plumber, car mechanic or fireman if we have frozen pipes, a broken-down vehicle or a raging inferno in our home. After all, this is urgent business about our property! But what about the more urgent business of our souls? The Bible says that each of us has both a body and a soul – the one being temporary and the other being eternal. How much attention do you give to each?

God also specifically reveals himself as the lord of destiny. In a rapidly changing world of global economic interdependence and ever-increasing geopolitical complexity, it is hard for us to attribute ultimate overarching power to any one being. Yet that is exactly the kind of sovereignty the Bible attributes to God. God has many titles in the Bible, including the first and last words of the Greek alphabet – Alpha and Omega, the beginning and the end. As H.G. Wells once said, "Until a man has found God, he begins at no beginning and ends at no end". But this is not only a matter of cosmology, about how the universe started and how it will ultimately end. God's power extends over the rise and fall of nations and regimes and to the destinies of individuals as well. God will judge all humankind (we will consider the question of heaven and hell in Chapter 8). These are profoundly important matters. I leave this anonymous quotation with you. "He who leaves God out of his reasoning does not know how to count."

Stumbling block number 2: The Bible

While it is God who will lead you to believe what the Bible says, I want you to understand why the Bible is my basic tool. The 66 books and letters in the Bible were written over a period of approximately 1,500 years that ended about 100 years after Jesus was crucified. The unity in its content impresses me as I see God's great salvation plan unfold. It was written under the guidance of the Spirit of God by a wide range of writers from different countries, cultures, social and educational backgrounds. It carries inherent authority and has been described as having a "divine impress". The genres in which the authors wrote are no less diverse – including history, poetry, prophecy, theology, romance and biography. The vast majority of these writers did not know each other, nor did they anticipate that their collective efforts would come to be known as "God's Word" and become the most widely read book of all time. One contemporary author has said of the Bible: "The Bible is the Word of God in the language of men – altogether divine, and yet at the same time truly human".[7]

Jesus Christ believed the Bible to be the Word of God, and successive generations of Christians have followed his lead. Jesus made many references to the truth of the law and the prophets in his preaching and explained that these writings all pointed to him as the source of eternal life. Even before the New Testament had been written Jesus drew attention to how vital its contents would be in calling people to have faith in him and in building the church. The Bible, then, has one overarching purpose – to enable God to reveal himself to humankind and, in doing so, to set out his great rescue plan for us all.

---

[7] Colin Peckman, *The Authenticity of the Bible* (Tain, Ross-shire: Christian Focus Publications, 1999), pp. 45–46.

In the past 150 years, modern archaeological research has enabled us to understand more about biblical events. We are wise to recognize that "Archaeology cannot prove the Bible to be the Word of God, but it establishes the Bible record, dismissing foolish arguments with foolish contempt . . . [archaeology's] unanswerable evidence helps makes the Scriptures better understood and more widely accepted by all, even by those scholars who only recognize pure science and place little or no value on the belief that the Bible is the Word of God".[8]

Food for thought:

Sometimes we are in two minds, not at all sure what we want. Someone once said, "I hope to resolve a central issue in my own life: how to reconcile the intellectual demands and pleasures of scientific thought with the sense of purpose and fulfilment that a rich spiritual life can provide."[9] Although this sounds optimistic and positive, sadly it was written by a man who totally excludes the possibility of the moral authority of God being asserted in all of us – a view radically at odds with the God of the Bible. What are the issues in your own mind that you need to resolve regarding God and the Bible?

---

[8] Peckman, *Authenticity*, p. 109.

[9] J.C. Advise, *The Genetic Gods: Evolution and Belief in Human Affairs* (Cambridge, MA: Harvard University Press, 2001), p. 104.

2

Where is God?

*"For God so loved the world that he gave his
only begotten Son, that whoever believes in him
shall not perish but have eternal life."*
(John 3:16)

Outline

Introduction: Is anything certain in this uncertain world?
God is.

Three biblical love stories: God's love is real and active in
human experience.

Stumbling blocks: On the way to understanding the Christian
message we encounter some complex issues: love and grace;
sin; and the cross and the resurrection.

Introduction

"You always know where to find her." "He's like clockwork." "You never have to guess what she's thinking." We often make remarks like these to describe a person's consistency and predictability – whether for good or ill, whether we find these characteristics beneficial or boring. You could have given any number of responses to the question in the first chapter, "Where am I?" And you might have given a very different answer ten years ago, or even last week, and I hope you will want to revise your answer at least a bit after finishing this book. But the answer to this chapter's question will always be the same, no matter when or where you ask it. God is consistently a God of love – indeed, love is his very essence. Perhaps the most well-known in the Bible, from John's Gospel, confirms this: "For God so loved the world that he gave his one and only Son, that whoever believes in him shall not perish but have eternal life" (John 3:16). As C.S. Lewis said, "Though our feelings come and go, God's love for us does not."

But we want to ask how we can be sure of God's love. For God, love is not a changeable emotion. It has no strings attached. God illustrates his love in actions that build relationships. Following are three stories, "biblical love stories", if you will, that demonstrate what God's love is like. The first story is about a loving father and an errant son – the former with a commitment to love without reserve, the latter with a desire to wander without consideration. The second story shows Jesus' insight into a woman's complex social life and his willingness to break through any barriers of convention in order to reach someone who wants to be forgiven. The third story explores the loving and patient relationship that God maintained with the nation of Israel, in spite of their hostility, forgetfulness and disbelief. You may reject him, but God loves unconditionally and for the long term. Following these three stories, we will look at three more stumbling blocks that prevent us from experiencing God's love towards us.

Three biblical love stories

1. The prodigal son

Jesus told this parable about a loving father's concern for his son, who had both offended him and left the family home.[10] This story illustrates God's love for all wanderers as well as his willingness to forgive.

Selfish parting. Unexpectedly, this father's younger son demanded his portion of the family estate. In this culture, such a request would have been tantamount to saying, "Dad, I wish you were dead." Further, the son would also have caused some financial embarrassment and perhaps hardship to his family, whose wealth would have been counted in flocks and who thus have been required to find liquid resources to share out. The son did not want to wait for his father's death but chose to live in the "now culture of youth". His gentle father agreed, but his sense of loss ran deep.

Wasteful wandering. The son planned to have a ball, and he did. He had no thought for the future but fulfilled his desire to exploit his new-found freedom in "wild living" – a phrase that leaves little to the imagination. The money quickly evaporated, and the local economy slid into famine. The glamour of the new adventure went the way of the fortune. The son ended up with a job feeding pigs – and the Jewish audience who first heard the story would have understood the desperation that entailed. Even worse, he would have been willing to eat the pigs' food if it had been on offer. He could sink no lower.

---

[10] Luke 15:11–32.

Sensible turning. The son had plenty of time among the pigs to think about his plight. Doubtless it was difficult for him to compare the bravado with which he left home with the stark reality of being in life's gutter. "What a loss of face," he might well have thought. "Everything about home looks good from this angle." Like everyone in his situation, "coming to his senses" was a necessary first step that would eventually lead to repentance and forgiveness.

Careful rehearsing. Now he needed words – or he thought he did. He may have rehearsed various ways of apologizing to his father. He would tell his father that he had sinned and didn't deserve to be regarded as a son, but that he was willing to be a servant – all the ingredients of self-effacing repentance. But he did not need words – only a repentant heart.

Uninhibited welcoming. In the most remarkable moment of the whole story, his father, who had been looking for his younger son daily since he left, spotted him from a distance and ran towards him with a compassionate welcome. Again, in the cultural setting, an elderly Jewish man behaving in such an uninhibited fashion spoke volumes about the love he had for his son and about the relationship with him that he longed for. It's a perfect reflection of God's love and longing for a relationship with all of us – if only we are willing to ask for forgiveness. The son made his rehearsed speech, but it was lost in the joyful and welcoming symbolism of his being given the best robe, a ring and a feast from his father. The father was celebrating nothing less than a return from death to life.

Angry recriminating. Returning home from the fields that day, the older son heard the music and dancing and took a very different view. When he learned the reason for the celebration, he became very angry. Doubtless there was a lot of history behind that anger. The older son had been obedient, consistent and loyal to his father. He had carried a heavy workload while his wasteful brother had scandalized the family by his behaviour. He refused even to go near his home under these circumstances.

Fatherly peacekeeping. The father came to the rescue again. He reassured his elder son that all of his wealth was his. This may have countered a lurking fear on the son's part that his father might show preferential treatment to his errant sibling. But the father was adamant that money and possessions would not crowd out the joy of a lost son being found. The younger son responded to his father's love, and a fractured relationship was mended. Over time the elder brother may have come to respect that – but the story leaves such questions unanswered.

2. The Samaritan woman

This incident from Jesus' ministry highlights his willingness to set aside differences in traditions and social practices in order to reach individuals.[11]

Eager to drink. Stopping off at a well at the end of a long journey, Jesus was both tired and thirsty. His disciples had gone into a neighbouring town to buy food. Jesus asked an unnamed Samaritan woman at the well for help to get a drink. She was drawing water for her own purposes and, from our perspective, Jesus' request seems unremarkable. As we will discover, however, there were several other dimensions to this conversation.

Query to answer. The woman picks up on the first of these undercurrents – Jews and Samaritans did not associate with each other. There had been a theological schism between

---

[11] John 4:7–26.

them for generations, and even a simple request for a drink of water was a step too far. Jesus refused to recognize or perpetuate such division – his mission was too great for that and his love too universal. While he was aware of the consequences that his contact with the woman might have in her local community and was sensitive to them, he had a deeper agenda.

Keen to explain. Jesus introduced the woman to information that she could scarcely have known. She may have heard of this new young prophet who was having such an impact on the countryside, but she would not have known that he was the Son of God. He brought her a mysterious counter offer of a different type of water – not for thirsty bodies, but for thirsting souls. Remarkably, this language struck a cord with this lady.

Dialogue to clarify. Jesus explained his identity and clarified what he was offering her. The woman commented that he had no container for water and no means of accessing it, given the depth of the well. But she was even more curious about where Jesus was going to get "living water" and what that did for the person who drank it. He explained that, although as a man he needed normal water, he was offering a totally different type of refreshment – not as a thirst quencher alone, but as a personal well of living water for each of us. Its remarkable properties include giving the thirsting soul eternal life – that life of quality and quantity that is nothing less than the life of God.

Request to change. Jesus handled this profound theology with a light touch and a simple metaphor, and in so doing whetted the woman's appetite for more. She badly wanted to have what Jesus had described, but there were aspects of her behaviour that had to be probed and changed. First she faced an honesty test.

Confession to make. Jesus asked her to go and get her husband, bring him to the well and join in this vital conversation. She confessed that she had no husband. Jesus confirmed that he knew this, and also that she had five previous husbands. The complex nature of her past is left to the reader's imagination. Jesus respected her transparency. It was necessary for anyone wanting to taste living water.

Prediction to understand. The woman was amazed by Jesus' knowledge of her private life and she acknowledged him as a prophet. Jesus pointed ahead to the end of disputes between Jews and Samaritans about where to worship – to the era we now know well, where God as a spirit is worshipped in spirit and truth. While the woman wistfully looked forward to hearing explanations of all such matters from the Messiah, Jesus made the remarkable declaration that she was now speaking to him. It was remarkable because he did not declare this with fanfare in a public place. In fact, he never did declare his identity in such a way – instead, the most public proclamation came from the lips of a dying man on a cross of shame.

3. The nation of Israel

The Old Testament tells the story of God's persistent love for his people, who in turn regularly ignored and discounted him. God acted throughout the different phases of their early history to demonstrate his love, care and faithfulness. What follows are just a few highlights from this long history that emphasize some important principles about God's love.

Creation. The first humans destroy, through their disobedience, the harmonious relationship between God and humankind. This sin establishes a lasting pattern. By Noah's time, the Bible tells us, God is already grieved by the people he put on earth (that didn't take long, you might think!). God preserves a select group through Noah, and God promises after the flood to never again send a flood to destroy all life.

Patriarchs. God intervenes in the affairs of humankind thereafter as his plan – to build a "great nation" set apart from others, especially by its unique relationship with God – unfolds through Abraham. In spite of being the holder of great promises, Abraham is disappointed with God because his wife's barrenness into her old age seems to indicate that she will not in fact mother this great nation. God did follow through on his promise to give Abraham and his wife Sarah a son, and Abraham demonstrated his great faith in God – not least by his willingness to sacrifice this son, Isaac. Joseph, Isaac's grandson, was mistreated by his brothers, sold into slavery and thrown into prison, but he experienced the goodness and love of God even through events that his brothers intended would harm him.

During the four hundred years or so between the events of Genesis and Exodus, the first two books of the Bible, God's "favoured" nation were slaves in Egypt – doubtless wondering for most of this time where this God who loved them was. God then raises up Moses to lead their rescue and escape and gives them ten dramatic displays of his power. Their escape from slavery through the Red Sea is a prelude to forty years of wandering in the desert. Although God cares for his people in the desert in amazing ways, the people little appreciate and regularly ignore the God who rescued them. Small wonder that God has been described as a "wounded" or "jilted" lover! Philip Yancey explains their blindness: "The Israelites give ample proof that signs may only addict us to signs, not to God."[12] On at least ten occasions in the desert

---

[12] Philip Yancey, *Seeing in the Dark: Faith in Times of Doubt* (Grand Rapids: Zondervan, 1988), p. 48.

the Israelites rebelled against God. Even when they finally reached the border of the promised new land of Canaan, and many times between Egypt and their destination, they longed for the "good old days" of their Egyptian past – yes, Egypt, where they were cruelly enslaved. Over these many years, the God of love's own people rebutted his love on a grand scale.

Kings. God's nation wanted to be like other nations and have a king. God gave them kings, if reluctantly. Illustrations from the lives of two of these kings, David and Solomon, reveal the relationship issues that emerged between them and God. The Bible summarizes David's reign as follows: "And David shepherded them [the nation] with integrity of heart; with skilful hands he led them."[13] Yet David, who loved God with all his heart, mind and soul, broke God's laws on a regular basis and in spectacular fashion. Like so many of us, he demonstrated that human beings are incapable of fulfilling a contract with God and receiving the promises and blessings that flow from obedience. Solomon, his son, followed him and commendably asked God for the blessing of wisdom. Halcyon days of prosperity followed, and with them a flourishing of artistic talent and temple-building in the nation. God appeared to be pleased with these developments and relieved that his people were at last returning his love. In a magnificent song at the dedication of the temple in Jerusalem, Solomon recognized that he had created an outstanding centre for worship, but that it had its limitations. "But will God really dwell on earth? The heavens, even the highest heaven, cannot contain you. How much less this temple I have built?"[14] Sadly, however, later in his life Solomon fell from these spiritual heights and from God's

---

[13] Psalm 78:72.
[14] 1 Kings 8:27.

favour. Among his crimes were adultery (on a grand scale) and the introduction of idol worship to God's holy city. Success by the measures of our world had crowded out his desire to praise God and lead a kingdom that would worship him. Many of the kings who followed Solomon never knew or obeyed God at all.

Prophets. Throughout this period of the kings, God sent messages to the nation via a long line of prophets. God displayed his power in dramatic ways through some of these prophets. Through Elijah, for example, a fireball on a mountain underlined God's pre-eminence. This had an immediate effect, but it did not last – either for the people or for the prophet himself. In his time, Isaiah also called on God to speak in the spectacular as he bemoaned the supremacy of evil in the world and the widespread suffering of the poor. "Truly you are a God who hides himself, O God and Saviour of Israel."[15] "Oh, that you would rend the heavens and come down, that the mountains would tremble before you!"[16] The problem throughout this whole period was not that God did not speak, nor was it that people did not hear him. People saw and heard God – through his prophets' words or by means of signs, wonders or miracles – but they chose to ignore and continue to disobey God.

Today, we see the coming of Jesus Christ against this background. After four hundred years of silence between the Old and New Testaments, God sent his message of love to humankind in the flesh. He sent his Son.

---

[15] Isaiah 45:15.

[16] Isaiah 64:1.

Reflection:

List some of the characteristics of God's love demonstrated in these three stories. How have you seen God's love at work in your own life?

While God gives us clear evidence throughout the Old Testament of his plan for his people, we see the ultimate evidence of God's plan and his love in Jesus Christ. "This is how God showed his love among us: He sent his one and only Son into the world that we might live through him. This is love: not that we loved God, but that he loved us and sent his Son as an atoning sacrifice for our sins."[17]

From New Testament times, the church has looked at one piece of evidence above all others to see the love of God in action. Here are two verses from a hymn written in 1707 by Isaac Watts that point to the significance of Jesus Christ.

When I survey the wondrous cross
On which the Prince of glory died
My richest gain I count but loss,
And pour contempt on all my pride.

Were the whole realm of nature mine,
That were a present far too small;
Love so amazing, so divine,
Demands my soul, my life, my all.

Stumbling blocks

Examining three more stumbling blocks will help us to see God's grace and love in a different way. It's amazing just how many people find such qualities in God unexpected and

---

[17] 1 John 4:9–10.

unnatural – so they can actually become a hindrance to faith. But we need to recognize not only that God loves, but also that he is holy – and so sin and its consequences are an awful reality in his reckoning. Finally, we look at love, grace and holiness all coming together at the cross and in the resurrection.

Stumbling block number 3: Grace and love

While sin is a stumbling block because people today view the concept of sin as unacceptable; grace and love can be stumbling blocks because we often don't expect them or think we deserve them. "Just look at my life – there's no way God could love me!" "I can't accept that I'm somehow part of a cosmic rescue mission – that sounds ridiculous." "I don't deserve it. So it might be for other people, but not for me." What's your own reaction to the idea that God loves you so much that he sent his Son to die to rescue you? Sin and grace are so closely connected that, without a consciousness of sin, you are unlikely to feel the need for grace. The story of the prodigal son and the woman at the well speaking to Jesus showed us the reality of recognizing and receiving grace only after repenting of wrongdoing. Karl Barth, a leading twentieth-century theologian, concluded after decades of study and reflection that the most accurate definition of God is "the one who loves". God's love is of the purest and deepest kind, far removed from the soiled images associated with the word today. Grace, a concept closely linked to love, is often described as "unmerited favour" towards a person. Nobody earns grace from God. It's free. It comes without conditions, catches or loopholes, and none of us can pay it back. It costs the giver everything, and the receiver nothing. So it was at the cross of Jesus Christ.

While this is all true, we may either know nothing about it or be content to ignore it. Many people investigating the claims of Christianity find incredible joy when, having become conscious of their own sinfulness, they discover that the God of the universe loves them. Many other highly intelligent and able people give God little attention until stress, family crises or major financial or career problems shatter their routine lives. On the other hand, there are those who ignore, or even despise, grace. "I don't need this. I didn't ask for it and I don't want it. Relationships founded on the unseen and invisible are far too flimsy for me. You'd have to be pretty desperate to want anything to do with these ideas." This last sentence is completely accurate – almost by accident. It is our understanding of how "desperate" we are before God that determines our behaviour. God wants to give us grace, but we have to receive it. He will not leave it on our doorstep like an unwanted package. Since God cannot under any circumstances treat evil as good, we need to confess our guilt before we get forgiveness. As the fourth-century theologian Augustine once said, "God gives where he finds empty hands". Have you ever held out empty hands to God?

The inextricable link between sin and grace is central to the message of the Bible. As Paul wrote, "For the wages of sin is death, but the gift of God is eternal life in Christ Jesus our Lord."[18] We will look at this gift in more detail later in the book, but here note the profound impact sin has on all of us when we view the world through God's eyes. God has provided a way to forgive our sin – but only at the phenomenal cost of the cross. So think about your need for grace and God's provision in these terms: "Grace means that there is nothing we can do to make God love us more. And

---

[18] Romans 6:23.

grace means that there is nothing we can do to make God love us less."[19] This is an incredible truth, given the indifference with which many of us treat God, and the lack of appreciation we show for all he has done.

When an individual finds Jesus, he or she is in turn commissioned to show the love received from God to others. I can only hope that you have experienced something of that love in your contact with Christians. As C.S. Lewis wrote, "To be a Christian means to forgive the inexcusable, because God has forgiven the inexcusable in you."[20]

While I hope that you are seeking Jesus even as you read this book, it may surprise you to learn that he is also actively seeking you. As a boy growing up in a semi-rural setting, I recall hearing my father's shrill whistle when it was time for me to return home. It was unmistakable. Even when I chose to ignore it – as I often did, to extend the time with my pals – they all recognized it and would shout to me. *"Neil! Your father has been calling for a long time!"* Your heavenly father has also been calling – using people, events and circumstances. Jesus told some parables about lost things (a son, a sheep and a coin), and they have the following in common: the sense of loss in the person searching; the great joy of rediscovery; and an ending of celebration. These are simple, but telling, glimpses of God in his search for us. He misses you as he searches for you. He will have great joy in reunion with you. *You* will be the cause of heavenly celebration! God then transforms each of us, as we shall see, and we learn the truth of the statement that "Christ accepts

[19] Philip Yancey, *What's So Amazing About Grace?* (Grand Rapids: Zondervan, 1997), p. 70.

[20] C.S. Lewis, "On Forgiveness", in *The Weight of Glory and Other Addresses* (New York: Collier Books/Macmillan, 1980), p. 125.

us as we are, but when he accepts us we cannot remain as we are."[21]

Reflection:

Richard Wilbur once said, "I die of thirst here at the fountain side". Why do you think it is that, with so much of God's love and grace on offer, we consume so little of it? How does it make you feel to know that God is seeking you?

Stumbling block number 4: Sin

Sin is one of the least popular words in the English language, and we rarely use it today – either because we reject the concept of sin, or because we prefer to use one of the many euphemisms to describe its symptoms. In recent times I have heard sin described as inappropriate conduct, emotional impairment, addiction, behavioural malfunctioning and so on. Most of the time, however, society regards sin as a "nameless given", a fact of life that is almost neutral and not to be talked about – certainly not in terms of blame. It is interesting, though, that when some monstrous evil confronts us (such as terrorism, child abuse or life-destroying sabotage), these euphemisms are inadequate to express our hostility and revulsion. We recognize and are willing to confront evil on a larger scale, but not any personal sins of which we might feel guilty. What's missing? The biblical answer is that we lack clarity regarding right and wrong. Moral guilt is a God-given sense that something is wrong. And we all have this sense, although we may either deny it or seek to destroy it. Many of us appear to be successful in both denying and destroying it.

---

[21] Walter Trobisch, *Love Yourself* (Downers Grove, IL: IVP, 1976), p. 26.

The words that the Bible uses for sin give us a clue as to how God regards it. The Bible describes sin, for example, as: "missing the mark"; "stepping over a known boundary"; "violation of a known law". All three of these examples assume the existence of a standard. Every society has a legal framework that includes codes, practices and standards that determine acceptable behaviour. But, in spiritual terms, the ultimate standards are God's – and herein lie the "stumbling block" qualities of sin. We live in a post-Christian society, so many people have rejected the traditional (biblical) standards but have not adopted new ones. We find it difficult, then, to accept the biblical truth that sin cannot approach God and God cannot tolerate sin. But the Bible is absolutely clear on this. God is the "most high", far above us in his holiness and majesty; he is "distant" from us until the work of Jesus unfolds and brings him near; he lives in "light and fire" of such intensity that by nature he is unapproachable – apart from Jesus. The Bible even graphically describes his distaste for, and violent reaction to, sin as leading him to vomit. These pictures do not sit at all well with most modern perceptions of God. People much prefer a benign, paternalistic image of God – not one that condemns all of us because of our sin.

While we avoid the subject of personal sin, every day we see evidence that people deny personal responsibility in any and every misdemeanour – from political spin, corruption and corporate crime to car theft, assault or fraud. But because of our attitudes to the concept of sin, we can deceive ourselves and view its effects with detachment. Philip Yancey comments, "In the modern world, sin approaches in camouflage. Too late do we realize that it blocks the way to shalom, to wholeness and health. We miss the hidden dangers that prompted the ancients to regard these sins as deadly."[22] The sins he refers to are pride, envy, anger, greed, sloth, gluttony and lust, and they are all built into our society in an unprecedented way. Indeed, our culture views some of them as virtues. For example, consumer-oriented societies regard "greed" in some forms as an essential driver, and "envy" is also an important element in the possession and replacement of material goods. Likewise "pride", even in aggressive forms, is a characteristic of idols and role models whose lifestyles are the envy of our youth. "Lust" has become a vast global industry, a dominant topic of conversation in many circles and a major component of the content of the World Wide Web.

Where does this leave you? Few of us would deny that we are guilty of wrongdoing in some form. Without accepting that we have committed what the Bible defines as sin, we cannot proceed very far in our search for Jesus. The Bible is clear that we are not just guilty of sin, but captive to it. You may say, "But my conscience is clear – at least most of the time." Few would go as far as to say, "I have no sense that I've ever done anything wrong. I never feel guilty." Conscience, however, is not always the best guide to guilt, since it becomes seared, hardened and insensitive to things that once generated guilt. At one extreme, the trials of mass murderers, perpetrators of genocide and similar acts clearly show this adaptation of the human conscience.

C.S. Lewis said, "We have a strange illusion that mere time cancels sin. But mere time does nothing either to the fact or to the guilt of sin." Sin makes God angry. The Bible demonstrates that love and justice are both vital components of his complex character. In order for us to relate to this just,

---

[22] Philip Yancey, *Rumors of Another World* (Grand Rapids: Zondervan, 2003), p. 106.

loving and holy God, therefore, his justice needs to be satisfied. But the Bible also makes it clear that we cannot solve this problem ourselves. Our situation, then, is this: "If we claim to be without sin, we deceive ourselves and the truth is not in us. If we confess our sins, he is faithful and just and will forgive us our sins and purify us from all unrighteousness."[23] The question we should ask, then, is "not why God finds it *difficult* to forgive, but how he finds it *possible* to do so at all."[24] But there is more.

The very heart of the biblical message is that God himself took all the initiative to make forgiveness possible. His own Son became the sacrifice necessary to satisfy justice on our behalf. "Christ loved us and gave himself up for us as a fragrant offering and sacrifice to God".[25] The writer of a New Testament letter to Jewish Christians linked the centuries-old requirement of animal sacrifice, as laid out in the Old Testament Law, to the one-off, unique sacrifice of Jesus Christ: "In fact, the law requires that nearly everything be cleansed with blood, and without the shedding of blood there is no forgiveness".[26] The good news of the gospel is that Jesus took on himself the curse of death, the consequence of our sin, so that we can have the blessing of new life. Listen to the power and assurance of these words from Paul. "This grace was given us in Christ Jesus before the beginning of time, but it has now been revealed through the appearing of our Saviour, Christ Jesus, who has destroyed death and has brought life and immortality to light through the gospel."[27]

---

[23] 1 John 1:8–9.

[24] John Stott, The Cross of Christ (Downers Grove, IL: IVP, 1986), p. 88.

[25] Ephesians 5:2.

[26] Hebrews 9:22.

[27] 2 Timothy 1:9–10.

We will continue to explore more about this amazing rescue mission and all of its benefits. You might still have unanswered questions about the biblical view of sin, since we have simply laid out the basic facts here. You might be asking, for example, "Why should *my* forgiveness depend on Jesus' death?" The biblical answer is twofold: first, God regards sin with deadly seriousness; and second, God is a God of majesty and holiness. On both counts, no lesser sacrifice would suffice. On another level, people often ask, "Why does God allow evil to exist in the first place?" The Bible brings us back to the original free choice of humankind to choose to disobey God, and all of the far-reaching consequences of that choice.

Reflection:

There's a lot to think about in this section. Take time to assess how close (or how distant) you are from God's view of sin and its consequences.

G.K. Chesterton once said, "Men do not differ much about what things they call evils; they differ enormously about what evils they will call excusable." Does our society's relative moral scale make sense to you? Why or why not?

Stumbling block number 5: The cross and the resurrection

At the cross where Jesus died, sin, grace and love all come together. Jesus' death on the cross and his subsequent resurrection are the central events of the Bible. Yet both were serious stumbling blocks for those investigating Christianity in biblical times, and they remain stumbling blocks for many today.

Death on a cross was considered shameful and cursed, and that someone claiming to be a saviour would die this way was humiliating. These were only some of the reasons for disbelief in Jesus' claims about his death. Meanwhile, mystery and incredulity surrounded his resurrection. The central point for us to remember is, as John Calvin said, that "in the cross of Christ, as in a splendid theatre, the incomparable goodness of God is set before the whole world." The four Gospel writers, Matthew, Mark, Luke and John, record for us the central teachings and events of Jesus' life. While they do not record details of ninety per cent of Jesus' life, they each devote fully one third of their accounts to the cross and related events before and after it. And they describe these events in forensic detail, with much drama and pathos.

Nobody rescues the hero. He dies alone and in shame. The promised Messiah's life ends in tragedy as he goes to the cross – which throughout his ministry was both the shadow behind and the goal ahead.

Why the cross? The cross was planned and executed as a rescue mission in which Jesus Christ delivered us from the weight of our sin and made forgiveness possible. The following four images help us to understand its full import. First, the cross is a *sacrifice* to appease anger – in this case God's anger, because of our sin. The cross is also a *payment*, as in a transaction in a slave market to free a slave. "For even the Son of Man did not come to be served, but to serve, and to give his life as a ransom for many."[28] Third, the cross *renews* the broken relationship between God and humankind, making communication possible again. Finally, the cross *mends* relationships, enabling us to come to God, as a family comes together after a period of strife and disagreement. Because the relationships have been repaired in this way, the church is described as a "community of hope", as people in

---

[28] Mark 10:45.

harmony with God and each other. How do these images help you view the cross in a new way? What do these images of the cross tell you about God? At the cross we see God demonstrating his justice, love, wisdom and power in equal measure. Indeed, the cross is so central to understanding who God is that John Stott, a Christian writer and theologian, says, "The cross assures us that this God is the reality within, behind and beyond the universe."[29]

Jesus suffered many injustices in the hours before his death. Buffeted alike by Jewish and Roman authorities, he was subjected to six interrogations in the course of twenty-four hours. No witnesses were called to his defence. No one who could expose his false accusers spoke up for him. His Father God remained silent. Herod, the Roman governor in Galilee, was deeply suspicious of Jesus. The Jewish leaders in Jerusalem, the Sanhedrin, wanted peace with their Roman masters at any price. The Jews had major theological disagreements with Jesus because he called God "Father" and claimed to have the power to forgive sin. Jesus refused to be drawn into the taunts of the crowd. But the high priest did evince a response. "'I charge you under oath by the living God: Tell us if you are the Christ, the Son of God.' 'Yes, it is as you say,' Jesus replied."[30] Jesus confesses at this final moment that he is indeed the Messiah.

The Romans reserved death by crucifixion for slave revolts, murderers and the like. Roman citizens who were to be executed were given vastly preferential treatment – they were beheaded. The Jews believed that anyone who was hung on a tree was cursed. What happened between Jesus and his Father on the cross is a profound mystery, but Jesus' anguished cry from the cross speaks volumes about his

---

[29] Stott, Cross, p. 226.
[30] Matthew 26:63–64.

painful separation. The shame associated with the cross was so shocking that Christians did not use it as a symbol of the faith until the fourth century under Constantine. But people recognized its profound significance immediately. Paul penned these powerful words to set it in context. "He [God] forgave us all our sins, having cancelled the written code, with its regulations, that was against us and that stood opposed to us; he took it away, nailing it to the cross. And having disarmed the powers and authorities, he made a public spectacle of them, triumphing over them by the cross."[31] To the apostles and the early church, Jesus' death and resurrection were gloriously triumphant events that would reshape the world. God's moral authority was supreme.

Jesus' resurrection tests the belief of many who accept the historic fact of the crucifixion. Yet those who claim true faith in Jesus must believe the fact of the resurrection as well. Why? Paul's answer is this. "And if Christ has not been raised, our preaching is useless and so is your faith. . . . And if Christ has not been raised, your faith is futile; you are still in your sins."[32] The resurrection is the very epicentre of belief.

The hours before the resurrection were incredibly difficult for the disciples. To a man, they had fled from the scene and were in hiding behind closed doors for fear of reprisals from the authorities. So, improbably in the culture of the day, the first witnesses to the resurrection were all women. Initially the disciples found their testimony hard to accept. But the risen Jesus Christ appeared about a dozen times subsequently, to some five hundred people. The impact of this event on Jesus' disciples was truly remarkable! The transformation from cowed and defeated followers to disciples

---

[31] Colossians 2:13–15.

[32] 1 Corinthians 15:14,17.

displaying outstanding bravery in their evangelism was astonishing. Ultimately, most of them were martyred for their faith. The evidence of the living Jesus fired them up for the rest of their lives as they played a vital part in establishing the early church. The resurrection was "not a belief that grew up within the church; it is a belief around which the church itself grew up and the 'given' upon which its faith is based."[33]

Perhaps you have already formed your views about the cross and the resurrection. You may still have some thinking, or even rethinking, to do. Jesus told Thomas, "Because you have seen me, you have believed; blessed are those who have not seen and yet have believed."[34] None of us can be eyewitnesses. But, by faith, all of us can become believers.

Food for thought:

How has your perspective changed regarding sin? And the cross and the resurrection? How would you explain these concepts to someone else who wanted to know what Christianity was all about?

Soren Kierkegaard said, "Christ has not only spoken to us by his life but he has also spoken to us by his death." How has Jesus Christ spoken to you through his death?

---

[33] C.H. Dodd, *The Founder of Christianity* (London: Macmillan, 1970), p. 163.
[34] John 20:29.

3

How will we meet?

"'The word is near you; it is in your mouth and in your heart,' that is, the word of faith we are proclaiming: That if you confess with your mouth, 'Jesus is Lord,' and believe in your heart that God raised him from the dead, you will be saved." (Romans 10:8–9)

Outline

Making the connection: How does God connect with human beings?

Stages of the journey: How have you tried, or are you trying, to connect with God? Where are you on the journey?

Life stories: God connects with individuals and families through a variety of circumstances and relationships.

Stumbling block: How does the Holy Spirit help us to meet with God?

Making the connection

God is faithful and constant; we are not. How, then, can we connect with God? People and circumstances can both play a key role in connecting us with God. You may have no expectation of relating to God in any way, or perhaps you cannot conceive of any circumstances that would lead to this happening. "I'm self-contained and can't imagine opening myself up to anything like confession and repentance – even if I thought that I needed to." "At certain points in my life I may have given God more attention, but these times never lasted. I'm not sure exactly why – I suppose normality kicks in as other pressures take over."

We can never predict how any one of us will come face-to-face with the issues that are on God's agenda. God doesn't work mechanistically or according to a formula. He created us all individually, and he speaks to us in different ways. He connects with many people through the big questions with which they wrestle. As you can see in Table 3.1, these issues can be incredibly diverse and stem from a wide range of experiences.

Table 3.1 If you could ask Jesus Christ any question, what would it be?

Why are there only seven days in the week?

How come life seems so unfair for a lot of people?

Did you really rise from the dead?

Since the majority of wars seem to me to be religious, what could he do to stop this?

Why am I here? – I need an answer to everything that's happened in my life.

Why are so many young people born disabled?

I think he answered them already – he has shown us that
Christianity is a good way of life.

Is there ever going to be peace on earth?

Was it worth it? Was it worth dying for us?

I have so many "why's" that I can't think of a single question.[35]

These questions all arose during street interviews about
different aspects of life conducted in London, Berlin, Zurich
and Helsinki. Some of these questions go to the heart of what
Christianity is about, while others are more peripheral. It is
interesting to note how many things people somehow
attribute to God – from disability, to the structure of the
week, to world peace. Men and women are looking for a
higher authority, but they find it difficult to specify who or
what this is – or who or what they want it to be! Other
responses in Table 3.1 are more overtly spiritual. Looking
for confirmation of Jesus' resurrection; the desire for an
explanation of the pattern of an individual's life; and "why's?"
are all crucial questions for people seeking Jesus. Two of the
questions stand out for me. First, posing the question "was
it worth it?" discloses a depth of thinking that is revealing.
The Bible addresses this specifically when it describes a
future time when Jesus will present his church, for whom he
died, to his Father – and it is indeed shown to be "worth it".
But the question is an entirely reasonable one to ask as we
see Jesus mocked and ignored, and God's will and moral
authority ridiculed. The second response that struck me is

---

[35] Source: Street interviews in European capitals, courtesy of Iain
Morris.

the claim that the questions have already been answered. Few of us could say that all of our questions about God have been answered – I know that I couldn't say that. And I still have honest doubts – but I have also more than enough certainty to believe and live a life of simple faith.

Reflection:

If you could ask Jesus Christ a question what would you ask? And why?

What questions regarding the Christian faith in general have you wrestled with over the years? Have any of them been answered to your satisfaction?

While you may well have many doubts at this stage, be encouraged by these words from Paul Tournier: "Where there is no longer any opportunity for doubt, there is no longer any opportunity for faith either".

Stages of the journey

In addition to the questions that we have, God also uses different people, events and circumstances to connect us to himself. Read through the various categories in Table 3.2 to determine where you fit. How are, or have, you and God been in touch? Who (or what) might link us to God will depend to some degree on your current circumstances and relationships. You may actually place yourself in the "missing" category: that is, you have no relationship, and have never had any relationship, with Christianity, Christians or the church. A large proportion of people in Western societies would describe themselves in this way. Having journeyed to this point in Chapter 3 together, however, my assumption is that you will find yourself somewhere in this table.

Table 3.2 Stages of the journey[36]

Stage	Characteristics
Practitioner	"Christian" in belief and practice, with clear evidence of both.
Casual	Has a nominal affiliation to a church and its traditions but does not practice or confess commitment to Jesus and has no desire to serve him.
Prodigal	Has drifted from the Christian faith but still uses the name and looks back with a mixture of cynicism and fondness. Often has a complex story of how it all happened.
Discoverer	Moving towards and exploring Christianity (often gradually), but doesn't yet use the name "Christian" for him or herself.
Challenger	Is strongly attracted to Jesus as a person, but doesn't fully accept Christian doctrine. Various stumbling blocks may hold him or her back.
Traveller	Atheist or agnostic, appears (and wants to appear) to be a long way from any interest in God.

Although there are large numbers of "casuals" in a post-Christian society, where people cling to tradition and respectability but not to God, these numbers have also declined rapidly. Family units are often two or three

---

[36] This table was inspired by comments made by C.S. Lewis in *Mere Christianity* (London/Glasgow: Fontana, 1955), p. 174.

generations from being "practitioners". Even such episodic associations with the church as weddings or funerals are progressively disappearing in favour of civil and secular ceremonies. I have seen relatively few "casuals" become "practitioners".

Although the prodigal's faith relationship with Jesus has already disintegrated, it may be years before this pulling away is fully evident in terms of their behaviours and attitudes. Each individual's story is complex. Some, for example, are emotionally torn between friendships in their old and new lives; others literally flee in the opposite direction, attracted by alleged new freedoms without moral constraints; still others lead double lives, behaving in certain circles as if nothing has changed. The population of prodigals increases all the time. I have witnessed in particular the grief of many Christian parents with prodigal children. God, however, is always ready to welcome back all prodigals. Both a change of will and an act of repentance are necessary to bring the prodigal and Jesus together again, but many prodigals seem to find these steps very difficult to take. As for all of us who come to Jesus, one of the prodigal's biggest hurdles is admitting that he or she has made mistakes. It can be painful, and even embarrassing, to admit that whatever course of action the prodigal took to split from fellowship with God, which once seemed attractive, was in fact a failure.

"Discoverers" have usually done a lot of thinking and research on different types of faith or on spirituality in a wider sense. Many have links with Christian churches. Others, like my father, are "discoverers" who simply read the Bible – in his case with no human guidance as to its meaning. When he was growing up there were no "practitioners" in his home. He searched for, and found, Jesus in his late teens. All the family did the same in subsequent years. And I found Jesus, too, because he was a "discoverer" some seventy-five years ago! It is not surprising that many people find God by reading his word. God designed it to happen like that. If you have not already begun reading the Bible, I recommend that you do so. Because of its power to transform lives, Christian communities across the globe dedicate untold effort and resources to studying, promoting and circulating the Bible. Conversions to Christian faith, especially in India and China, have been occurring on a truly remarkable scale in recent years. In such contexts, and particularly in Islamic countries, traditions, social mores, family and peer pressures can make conversion costly and painful. Most of us cannot begin to comprehend the challenges they face.

"Challengers" can be quite restless and may have problems with stumbling blocks like the ones we have been examining. Some challengers enjoy finding obscure semantic or doctrinal issues to quibble over. The "challenges" they present may also be simple excuses for inertia. In short, they may be going somewhere – or they may be going nowhere at all in an alleged search for Jesus. The key here is the challenger's attraction to Jesus. When that desire to know Jesus becomes strong enough, these issues disappear. People do also come to faith in Jesus with continuing doubts and uncertainties, however. Augustine, a faithful follower of Jesus Christ from long ago, once said, "I wish to be made just as certain of things that I could not see, as I was that seven and three made ten".

Finally, there are "travellers" – who might not even be aware that they are on a journey. While he was neither an atheist nor an agnostic, Paul the apostle (we will look at his story in Chapter 7) was a "traveller" who turned from his Jewish religiosity to a personal faith in Jesus. People at this stage on the journey often have well-developed defence mechanisms to close out spiritual truth. But the Spirit of God will never give up trying to connect with all people, everywhere – regardless of where they are spiritually.

Reflection:

Can you identify any occasions in recent years when people or circumstances made you more aware of God? How did you respond? Have you ever tried to connect with God? What happened? If you felt that you failed, did you talk to anyone about this?

Life stories

Following are four stories about people who were prompted by people, events and/or circumstances to think about God. As you read these accounts of fictional characters in real-life situations, reflect on similarities and differences with your own circumstances and attitudes.

Robert Hardman: Life in the midst of death. "It makes you think," Robert observed as, seated at his impressive executive desk, he read the newspaper headlines over his morning coffee. Robert was a self-contained, independent-minded senior advertising man. Creativity and innovation were his business, and he was good at it. He didn't like it when external events disrupted his thoughts. The obituary column in *The Times* that day featured three tributes to people he knew. One was a school friend who had become an eye specialist of great repute and had devoted many years and a lot of his wealth to establishing clinics in the poorer parts of Africa. He had died tragically in a car accident in Cairo, aged 45, leaving a wife and four children. "How could God let this happen to a man like him?" The second was a man he once worked with in a leading agency in Paris. The tribute was glowing. "He probably wrote it himself," Robert mused. He had had good reasons not to trust this man, and his death only touched Robert because of the chronic illness he knew this man had suffered. Why, Robert wondered, was such pain allowed? (By God? He assumed it must be God.) The final obituary he read stirred his thoughts for very different reasons. Mrs. Helen Wright, a neighbour in her late eighties, had been a quiet, unassuming lady. Robert was astonished to read that she had left her £5 million fortune to a variety of Christian causes. The amount of money blew his mind, for her lifestyle had been very modest. The allocation of the fortune totally baffled him. "Just think of what I could do with money like that! What a waste!"

Over his second cup of coffee, it suddenly struck Robert that in the space of an hour he had twice blamed God for events and also questioned the sanity of another person who lived by different standards. He knew that he had no right to question Mrs. Wright's good judgment, and he had no confidence that there was even a God – but who else could one turn to with life and death questions like those? He began to wonder if there was more to life. Robert was a bit annoyed that thoughts of God kept creeping back into his mind over the next few days – for the first time ever. "Maybe I'm just getting older, but maybe I should really try to find out what life is all about. But I don't even know where I'd start."

He started by going to Mrs. Wright's funeral two days later. He had never set foot in the church before and was slightly embarrassed. The building was packed, and he slipped in at the back. This funeral service turned out to be one of the most amazing experiences of his life. He heard about Mrs. Wright's strong faith during a long life of adversity. He could feel the love that the mourners shared for her. And they sang as if they were celebrating, not mourning! The congregation was rejoicing in the triumph of God in her life. Robert was profoundly moved – and ashamed of the attitude he had when he first read the tribute to her in the press. Before he left the church, he dropped into their bookshop and bought his first Bible and a few other books. He was determined to find out more about the role of God in the world. He knew that he had some deep thinking to do. He felt a deep conviction that, so far in his life, he had only managed to combine success, superficiality and shallowness.

Jeremy Wallace: Witnesses a family transformation. Jeremy Wallace was a man with some unique talents. He had built up a highly successful public company – which had rewarded his shareholders and added to his considerable personal wealth. Not only did Jeremy have "hands on" business skills, he also combined them with an intense interest in all things artistic. He felt as much at home on the boards of art museums and opera companies as he did in trade associations and high-level negotiations with government bodies. As part of his community interests, he attended a church which was noted for the quality of its music and for its social networks. The latter was probably his primary motivation for attending (although he might not admit it). In his characteristically clinical way he told his friends, "Church is properly positioned in my priorities – it's not too demanding at either a personal or financial level. And that's exactly as it should be."

And then something dramatic happened in his family – something for which he was totally unprepared. Fiona, his only child, was in her late twenties. She was his pride and joy, and the very model of what Jeremy wanted her to be. She was rapidly climbing the career ladder in a prestigious investment bank with a glittering future before her. Fiona's church involvement mirrored that of her father – passive, socially compliant and undemanding. It did, that is, until she moved to a nearby city to further her career and began to share a flat with two girls who introduced her to a very different way of practising Christianity. It was what they did rather than what they said. They lived their lives with Jesus and his teaching at the centre. They weren't killjoys, but they did spend time reading the Bible and praying each day. Their focus and discipline appealed to Fiona's ordered, professional mind. Over a period of many months, Fiona (in Jeremy's words) "caught religion". She began to talk about how much she enjoyed her personal faith in, and her obedience to, Jesus. She started to witness to her family about this new sense of meaning and reality she had found.

Jeremy was baffled by how happy and content she was, but he was also torn. At one level, Fiona had the right to choose her own way. But having such a committed (and different) family member was both disconcerting and disruptive. After all, he had shown her an "acceptable" way to be a Christian – and she had rejected it. He tried to avoid the subject with her and her probing questions. "Dad, what does God mean to you? Why do you bother going to church at all?" she would ask. "Has the Spirit of God ever spoken to you?"

Jeremy was a confident, fearless, arrogant man, and he didn't like these questions. But he knew that something life-changing had happened to his beloved daughter and he didn't want to lose her. He felt how sharply her vibrancy, peace and contentment contrasted with his restless existence. He admitted to himself that her questions were valid, and he privately sought out some Christians to ask them about what had happened to his Fiona. Because she clearly had something he had never dreamed of, subtly (and improbably) Jeremy became more aware of himself as a self-contained cynic living within his own ordered world – and he began to seek God. God broke through to reveal to Jeremy that what he was witnessing was the transforming power of the gospel in his own family. He maintained, however, that it was improbable that this could ever happen to him.

Carol Ann Cook: Failure on the way to triumph. Failure was not a word that featured in Carol Ann's vocabulary. She had never experienced failure at a social, academic or personal level. A brilliant student of politics and economics, and the daughter of a family whose fortune had been made in mining over three generations, she had studied at some of the finest schools in the world – London School of Economics, the Sorbonne and Harvard. She was active in political pressure groups of the centre left, but she impressed many by her willingness to engage in pioneering social work in inner urban communities. There she showed great consistency of purpose, an uncanny ability to relate to many different client groups, and considerable bravery in the face of danger. It was clear that her heart was in trying to exert influence over local and national politics in favour of such groups. After five years as a local politician and three as a political adviser, she was selected to stand as a member of the UK Parliament for an inner urban constituency in the Midlands. Carol Ann won support through bitter debate and stiff opposition from some local activists. "How can someone with her wealth and credentials be credible on the streets?" "It's easy for the upper classes to posture about deprivation, but it never lasts." "We would look like fools with her as our chosen candidate!" But she was chosen, and as the election date approached the local political climate became ever more heated. Several independent candidates stood against her and succeeded in splitting the large local vote. The other candidates also gave lots of ammunition to her political opponents. The election night was one of the worst in her life. She lost the election by a large majority. She felt deceived, let down and, for the first time in her life, she saw herself as a failure. She had selflessly invested almost twelve years of her life in this poor district – to no effect. Many shared her shock at the outcome and her deep sense of injustice. "Carol Ann's critics have had years to express their views about her background, and every single one of them experienced her unswerving commitment to the area. Why destroy her now?" demanded one of her supporters. But where did Carol Ann go from here?

It took many weeks for her to calm down, and her sense of being a failure continued to plague her. Then, one day, she found treasure in her attic – in the improbable form of a graduate paper on political failure that she had written in Paris while at the Sorbonne. It was entitled, "Failures on the way to triumph". She couldn't remember why, but she had written about a number of religious leaders whose lives had challenged the political and social systems of their day. Jesus Christ, Ghandi and Martin Luther King were among them. For some reason, her thoughts focused particularly on Jesus. She had included a great number of references to the Bible in her paper. The most powerful empire in the world and a sophisticated religious system were both aligned against Jesus – a man without support structures, resources or reliable followers. To his contemporaries, his death looked like a total disaster and shameful far beyond anything she had experienced. Yet, as she read on, she saw with new eyes the disaster of death become the victory and triumph of resurrection. While she had little biblical knowledge, she was a trained scholar and fair-minded. She wondered why she continued to think about Jesus, rather than the titanic struggles for voting rights for women or for racial equality that were so central to her work for social change. She went on to investigate the life of Jesus in some detail. She saw his social concern and care for the weak, but she also saw something else. When she studied his teaching, she read of a new way of life that was founded on his death and was a reform from the inside. This attracted her intellectually but, more importantly, it challenged her personally. She knew that what she was reading was dynamite and life-changing – and she wanted her failure to be transformed into a new life of faith.

John and Marcia Russell: Speaking through relationships. John and Marcia and their two children (Mary, 12 and Darren, 10) were natural "joiners". They loved family events and looked for every opportunity to help their children integrate with the community, develop social skills and follow their natural interests in sport. Neither John nor Marcia had had these opportunities as children. John's parents were rather reclusive, and Marcia's had been older and often in poor health. The one organization that the Russell family had not joined was a church. If asked why, John would say that he could not see any real benefit in it, recalling rowdy sessions in school assemblies when the aged chaplain visited. "We're already doing lots of things to enrich our family and it's great – maybe sometime."

But the Russells had viewed their arrangements as if nothing was likely to change as the children, and they themselves, developed different interests. For example, John's initial devotion to judo was much curtailed by persistent back injuries and he became more involved with the swimming group at the sports centre. Marcia continued with her aerobics, and her close-knit team extended their social interaction well beyond the club. She found this a highly supportive group in all the different dimensions of her family life. As she told John, "Not all of our family units are stable, and even we have our moments as a couple. Sharing experiences is invaluable."

Indeed it was a supportive group, but it went much further than domestic matters. For example, Anna was a spiritualist with a perspective on life that scared Marcia at times; Shona was a third-generation immigrant who practiced the Muslim faith and had an interest in comparative religion; while Michelle and Liz were actively involved in a local evangelical Christian church, which was much admired for its commitment to the community. Marcia absorbed all of this and actively participated in many interesting conversations about "faith" – a concept that was almost entirely new to her. It was both surprising and refreshing, because Michelle and Liz (both senior medical professionals) showed a simplicity in their personal trust in Jesus Christ that reminded her very much of the early behaviour of her own children towards John and her. As she said to John, "I thought that education, science and rational thinking would have removed the need for faith, but this is unbelievably real for Michelle and Liz. They've even told me several times that they're praying that we will seek and find Jesus for ourselves." John was not impressed and commented that it was fine for women but not for real, independent men! This infuriated Marcia, but John had to admit to himself that these conversations with her Christian friends had made a profound impact on his wife – who was neither an impressionable nor naïve person.

John and Marcia's children were in the same badminton club with Michelle's children and had become good friends. The families ended up meeting regularly for pizza after their practices and their relationships grew and deepened. Eventually both John and Marcia started attending a class in the sports centre to learn more about the Christian faith. For the first time, they realized that there were big life questions to which they needed answers. They found that meeting with friends with whom they were comfortable was the best way to find these answers. They did just that, and Marcia saw her need to place her faith in Jesus first. John followed suit six months later, after a prolonged struggle with his pride.

Reflection:

If you see yourself, or anyone you know, in similar circumstances or with similar attitudes, what can you learn from these stories?

Stumbling Block

Stumbling block number 6: The Holy Spirit

How would you explain the interweaving of circumstances, events and relationships in the stories above that brought each of these people to consider God? The Bible tells us that this is part of the work of the Holy Spirit. The Holy Spirit is the third Person of the Trinity, comprising the Father, the Son and the Spirit. Understanding the Holy Spirit can be a stumbling block in part because of the logical and theological conundrum (how can God be one God in three Persons?), and in part because of the mystery surrounding how the Holy Spirit lives in us and speaks to our hearts and minds. Without minimizing the theological complexities, for our purposes we will focus on two key aspects of the Spirit's work. First, part of his "job description" is to convict and convince all of us about the truth of God and our own sinfulness. We don't invite him to do this, and most of the time we may not even be aware of it until, as in the stories above, something breaks into our consciousness. Like the atmosphere full of satellite signals, we can't receive spiritual signals when our equipment is tuned off or tuned in to other imperatives. Times of crisis or change often enable us to tune in properly, to be aware of the bigger picture of what is happening in and around us.

We learn about the second part of the Spirit's work from Jesus' promise to his disciples. As he announced that he would be leaving them soon, Jesus told the stunned disciples: "And I will ask the Father, and he will give you another Counsellor to be with you for ever – the Spirit of truth. The world cannot accept him, because it neither sees him nor knows him. But you know him, for he lives with you and will be in you."[37] Having convicted and convinced someone about their need for God, the Spirit remains with the believer to help him or her live out that faith. The Greek word for "counsellor" used here refers to "one who stands by the side", such as an advocate or defence lawyer. The word also sometimes described a "cheerleader" in a battle. The Spirit's work is *not* to reconstruct the Christian's personality – because God created us and uses what we offer him. The Spirit's aim, rather, is to encourage the growth of the fruit of the Spirit (godly character) in our lives: "love, joy, peace, patience, kindness, goodness, faithfulness, gentleness and self-control."[38] What a different place our world would be if more of these virtues were evident! Note that the fruit is singular – like an orange with nine segments. Christians cannot choose to have peace, for example, or gentleness – they are all complementary and are to be interwoven in our lives. The various words used to describe the Spirit (Comforter, Counsellor and Helper) suggest that he aids the

[37] John 14:16–17.
[38] Galatians 5:22–23.

Christian through a gradual process of change, with many ups and downs – and that he does so with understanding and love. The promise that the Spirit will come to dwell in every Christian is a central promise of the faith. It is impossible for a Christian to maintain faith and hope and focus on Jesus in a broken world without such divine assurance and power. This biblical promise is actually a "guarantee" – a sure and secure promise for the future.

The Christian life is not an easy one and, regardless of their age, experience and circumstances, all Christians everywhere declare their constant need for the Spirit's help. Such is the apparent irony and God's wise design that we need God to enable us to be godly. I have found the following verse profoundly reassuring, for example, as I write this book in my current circumstances: "The Spirit helps us in our weakness. We do not know what to pray for, but the Spirit himself intercedes for us with groans that words cannot express."[39] Or, as the popular Christian writer Philip Yancey says, "When we don't know what to pray, the Spirit fills in the blanks."[40]

Reflection:

Take a few minutes to describe how your life would be different if the fruit of the Spirit was evident in what you do, say and think.

---

[39] Romans 8:26.
[40] Yancey, *What's so Amazing?*, p. 153.

Food for thought:

The sceptic Arthur Koestler once said that "God seems to have left the receiver off the hook, and time is running out." Have you ever felt that this is true?

Jot down a brief description of all the times in your life when you felt some sort of awareness of God – whether you blamed him for something, were questioning him, saw a glimpse of his love or power in a person or situation, or even yearned for him when you felt he was absent.

II

Stepping Stones

4

What's missing in my life?

"The agnostic believes no one can know. The hedonist doesn't care to know. Atheists believe there is nothing to know." Max Lucado[41]

Outline

Do voids exist? While we all wish things were different sometimes, if we can see beneath our discontent we will find the heart of the problem: the voids of the heart.

What's missing? We answer serious questions about what's missing in our lives at different levels. Four different life stories help us to determine what's missing in our own lives.

From stumbling blocks to stepping stones: How can the stumbling blocks that stand in the way of faith become stepping stones to help us to understand more about who God is?

---

[41] Max Lucado, *Next Door Savior* (Nashville: Word, 2003), p. 132.

Do voids exist?

We all use literal and metaphorical stepping stones every day – to cross a stream without getting our feet wet or to navigate through difficult ground in relationships, business or politics. We choose stepping stones with care, knowing that they need to be stable enough to hold the full weight of the problem. So it is on this journey to faith. But we have to know where we're going, and how far, before stepping stones will be of any use to us.

So we begin by looking at the emptiness many of us feel when we survey our achievements, successes and failures. Many of us have, at one time or another, made the following kinds of statements. "I don't have any job satisfaction, and I really need a change. I get this empty, unfulfilled feeling every time I come to work." "There's something missing in our family. It seems we always need just a little more money to make us content." "The world is a complete mess. It makes me depressed and frustrated – but what can I do?" "Some Christians I know put me to shame. They have some sort of 'x-factor' in their lives. If it could be bottled, I'd drink it. I really respect them, but I'd never have the stamina or willpower to live like that." These remarks communicate genuine emotions and needs, but they are not actually addressing the heart of the problem.

But what are the real voids of the heart underneath these problems? Often these are so hidden that someone close to us can have such a void and we may never know. For example, a couple longing for a child, unable to have one and unwilling to talk to anyone about it, may have just such an aching void; as might a single person who has never found a life partner; or someone with an unfulfilled ambition.

Whether it reflected a true void of the heart I can't say, but I am reminded of the discontented Marie Antoinette who, from the opulence of the French court in the eighteenth century, lamented, "I have everything, but nothing tastes." King David expressed a true void of the heart in the Psalms. He wrote these words as an exile, with an intense longing to be back in his own country in God's presence at the magnificent temple in Jerusalem. "My soul yearns, even faints, for the courts of the LORD; my heart and my flesh cry out for the living God."[42] David perfectly captures the depth of human longing for relationship with God. Such words from the heart have a distinctive quality and intensity. People often come to the end of their search for God when they discover that they have a permanent emptiness in their hearts. For example, they may long for peace when their minds are restless and troubled by all the cares of their lives. They may look to the future with fear. They may despair of ever finding anything that is real and lasting, having attained so many goals that prove to be ultimately transitory and unsatisfying. I have seen people literally come to their wit's end and publicly cry out to God in desperation for forgiveness. I have seen addictions, terminal illness, even the illusion of success itself, drive people to realize that only God can fill these voids.

Reflection:

What would you identify as the voids in your life – now or in the past? Have some or all of them been filled? If so, how?

What's missing?

Is there anything missing in your life? Table 4.1 encourages you to do some soul-searching. We have all had the experience of asking someone a question and not getting the full answer immediately. Sometimes there's simply not

---

[42] Psalm 84:2.

enough time to go into the details, sometimes those details are too personal or revealing and so on. We answer questions at different levels according to circumstances. At what level will you answer this question:

Table 4.1 Is there anything missing in your life?

Level	Response	Comment
1	Nothing is missing from my life.	First-level, casual, perhaps superficial response. Few people want to admit gaps they can't fill by their own efforts. At this surface level, people may not consider the spiritual dimensions of life at all.
2	I need more of almost everything.	We rarely hear these words spoken, since few would admit to the underlying sentiment. But this desire drives our consumer society and culture, whether explicitly or implicitly. Many people feel that they are missing many things, but God is not likely to be one of them.
3	I want explanations for things I don't understand.	This more cerebral and (potentially) spiritual response asks "why": why ill-health, death, misfortune, evil, crime, injustice, and so on?
4	I don't know whether there is a higher divine authority.	This is the heart of the matter for many people. Some of us don't always (or ever) acknowledge that this is what is missing from our lives, but it is perhaps a part of all our consciences by design. The questions that prompt this response include: "Why am I here?" "Where is the world going?" "Is there life after death?"

At what level will you answer the question – either in conversation, or privately within yourself? Level 1 is an initial, almost knee-jerk, response – especially from prosperous and self-sufficient people. If such people find something is missing they fill it, since the gap can often be closed by new activity, different social contacts, more leisure and so on. The second level of response is rarely spoken, and we can detect it more from what people do than from what they say. Behavioural patterns suggest that this is the answer many people would give if they were being honest with themselves. The third level of response is more serious. It is usually the consequence of a crisis and begins to touch on some personal matters. "Why?" is invariably a cry of anguish, and it often involves the search for simple answers to complex questions. Impatience and frustration can often follow. On occasion people direct these feelings, often in anger, towards God or some other imagined higher authority. The fourth level of response gets at the central issue and is perhaps at the back of every human mind, since it asks life's biggest questions. The following four case studies explore each of the levels of response.

1. Nothing is missing from my life: The Buchanans' prosperity

Mary and John Buchanan lived in an eighteenth-century mansion located in one of country's finest villages. They were enjoying their day at a new shopping complex – a splendid facility full of designer shops with a wide range of specialist leisure services for all ages. Set on a vast site which had been regenerated following the closure of a steel-making plant, this complex celebrated the economic success of the whole region. It was a beautiful day and, as they strolled around, they shared a deep sense of well-being. They were both in their mid-fifties, in good health and were very comfortable financially. They had a fine family in stable relationships and many friends. They also enjoyed cruises, memberships in prestigious golf clubs, and a villa in Spain . . . what more could anybody want?

As they sipped their favourite café latte in a garden bar, Mary, a gentler and more reflective person than her husband, commented, "We've been very lucky."

"True," John said, "but I've worked for every penny we have. It's been a hard and tough road, and I've had to be a bit ruthless at times – but my conscience is clear." John had made his fortune as a commodity trader specializing in copper futures and had been semi-retired for years. He had worked since on managing his investments.

Shortly after that pleasant outing, John was travelling by rail to meet one of his financial advisers in London. Putting aside the papers for the meeting, and with a warm feeling of financial security, he struck up a casual conversation with an army colonel, Ernest Malcolm, with whom he was sharing the carriage. Both men were excellent conversationalists, and their topics ranged from world affairs and politics, to careers and families. John was thoroughly enjoying the journey. Their talk turned to more philosophical issues, and on these Ernest had much more developed thoughts than John. John quietly mused that the pursuit of success had narrowed his interests, even though it had greatly sharpened his mind. Ernest asked him, "What else would you want in your life that you don't have?" A year ago John might have said a grandchild – but now he had two lovely granddaughters. "I can't really think of anything that's missing – why do you ask?" Ernest took a moment to respond. "Well, I suspect that you've answered my question in terms of material and tangible things – as many people would. But what about spiritual considerations? For example, what role does God play in your life?" An honest answer from John would have been "none at all", but he chose the defensive route and started to explain his impressive charity work. They parted soon after – but Ernest's question continued to simmer in John's conscience, as did the quizzical look on Ernest's face as he had struggled to answer it.

Over dinner that evening John told Mary about this conversation. She listened carefully and surprised him by saying, "I think we need to be able to answer his question, John. There is something missing. Even if you don't recognize it, I feel that having more is simply not enough anymore. I think the colonel's question is very important." John didn't sleep well that night. He had given a poor answer to Ernest's question, and he needed to know what was really behind it. The next morning, he told Mary that he was going to call Ernest Malcolm and arrange to meet him to talk further.

2. I need more of almost everything: The Harrison family struggles

Stephen and Avril Harrison had five children between the ages of five and fifteen – two from their own marriage, and three from previous marriages. Both parents worked long hours to pay the bills and were also very committed to spending quality time with the family. Stephen and Avril were amazed at the influence that the children's peers had on their preferences for clothes, shoes, bicycles and so on. They felt a certain amount of pressure because some of their children's friends came from affluent homes. Stephen was very open about this situation with Shaun (age 15) and Sally (14), the two older children. "We'll always do our best for you, but we just can't afford to have everything the neighbours do." Stephen didn't mention the continuing cost of his divorce settlement, as he thought this was an unreasonable burden to place on the children.

The Harrison family would have agreed, thinking solely in material terms, that they needed more of almost everything – a bigger income, house, garden, car and so on. Stephen and Avril realized that there were many families in their own town whose financial position was much worse than theirs. They tried to teach their children to take care of what they had, to be content and to understand the value of money.

Stephen and Avril talked a great deal about these issues because they saw no solution to their financial position. Especially as the children grew older, Avril would make comments like, "We need to teach the children a different value system. They need to understand that there are other things in life which are much more important than possessions, such as honesty, kindness, care for others . . ." But neither Stephen nor Avril had really thought through what a different value system might look like. They generally described themselves as liberal and as passive supporters of socialist ideas dating from their student days. But this fell short of a set of principles they could teach their children. Besides, Avril had begun to think about how such change occurs – was it from the inside or the outside? Did motivation for behaviour really have to stem from a deeper, spiritual conviction? Stephen and Avril regarded themselves as decent and honourable people (and others who knew them felt the same). But were they giving their children a chance by not teaching them about spiritual issues? After all, this "more of everything" culture would probably dominate their lives more than it ever did the lives of their parents. But Avril wondered how one would ever begin to try to find answers to these questions in the busyness of life.

Both Stephen and Avril were IT specialists and used the internet for all sorts of transactions. One evening Avril plugged some key words, reflecting the values that they wanted to teach their family, into a search engine. She came up with several philosophies and, to her surprise (since she had no religious background at all), many links to Christian churches and organizations. She was even more surprised to find that there were several churches in their neighbourhood teaching exactly the kind of values they'd been thinking about. Now that they knew where to look, their search intensified. They bought, and began to read, the Bible. They were amazed by its fresh and challenging message and ideas that really struck a chord with them. Not long afterwards, the family began attending a local church whose leadership team included a fine pastor who gently guided them to faith in Jesus. They have great excitement in their new-found faith and in being able to teach their children a value system that stems from a faith that makes sense of their whole lives – their relationships, justice, love, forgiveness, life and death, as well as material possessions.

3. I want explanations for things I don't understand: The Philip Masterson tragedy

Professor Philip Masterson was one of the best paediatricians of his generation. Highly regarded by his peers across the globe, he fought hard to be able to devote his time and resources to what he knew in his heart he wanted to do – namely, to look after children. In order to do this as well as help bring up his own seven children with his wife Annette, he kept professional committee work and travel to prestigious international conferences to a minimum.

Philip worked in a large and extremely busy city hospital. He led a centre of excellence, but in a "hands-on" way. He enjoyed the challenges of complex surgery, but he also found his clinics very rewarding – watching the children progress to health and the families delight in their recovery. Many sang his praises. "He's one of the finest physicians I have ever known. He has an astonishing understanding of children." "He has an incredible gift to comfort children and tell them what is happening in their own language." While Philip's patience with children seemed infinite, his intolerance of hospital bureaucracy was legendary. He put constant pressure on administrators and government ministers for more resources to run his unit better and to improve patient care. His reputation in the wider community and his charismatic personality made him an outstanding fundraiser. As a result, his unit was one of the best-equipped in the country – but funding for staff was still inadequate in his view, hence he pressed for more.

Philip Masterson always went "the extra mile" when it came to patient care and follow-up. Simon de Villiers was a seven year old boy with a malfunctioning heart and recurring kidney problems. Philip had operated on him three different times, and each operation had had its own special risks. Simon was a lovely, cheerful child who handled these difficulties astonishingly well. He was also the son of his friend and anaesthetist colleague, Henry de Villiers. One Friday night, after an exhausting week, Philip decided to drop into the de Villiers home to see how Simon was progressing. En route he passed through a dangerous neighbourhood, where car crime was rife. A sudden pull on his steering wheel indicated that he had a puncture, and he pulled off the road to investigate. The area seemed quiet enough, so rather than call for assistance on his mobile he proceeded to change the tyre on his Mercedes.

He had almost completed the task when a gang of passing youths, high on alcohol and drugs, attacked him. In the tussle that ensued, he sustained a fierce blow on the head from a baseball bat. He died of a brain haemorrhage, aged forty-six, some twenty-four hours later. The community reacted with outrage, and the attack was condemned from every quarter. "How could a bunch of drunken teenage thugs snuff out such dedication, skill and experience?" the local press demanded. The media expressed many such hostile comments about the case for days to come. But the tragedy aroused deeper feelings. Editorial columns carried thoughtful pieces about how evil could destroy goodness. Why, they asked, were such things allowed to happen? Where would all this lead? And could God (or someone) not intervene to protect the good? Many people eloquently expanded upon these sentiments at Philip's memorial service some three weeks later. Over three thousand people attended the city cathedral for a memorable celebration of the life of a fine father, a great physician and a distinguished citizen. Many who attended were in their teens and twenties – grateful former patients. While it was an uplifting event and a superb tribute to Philip, there was little hope – and a lot of anger over the waste of a life in its prime. There were also many unanswered questions, and few people knew where to look for solutions. Some blamed God for falling asleep on the job.

As the cathedral emptied, many were visibly moved by the occasion, but in different ways. One group went off to pray for an explanation that Philip's family would understand. Another individual left with a renewed passion to devote his life to helping the types of young people who commit such crimes. Still another of his Christian colleagues went off to ask God that he might be better able to understand and accept his sovereign will. But many, many more left asking, "Why?".

Reflection:

Many wrestle with the question "why?" in similar circumstances. While Christians may also ask this question, the Bible is clear that God is in control – even when we don't understand or see a purpose for things that happen. The Bible emphasizes that our response is to be one of faith – however difficult that may be. Would we be better sufferers if we knew and were able to understand the reason behind our suffering? I doubt it – although I understand that the absence of what is seen as the "comfort" of definitive "answers" can cause great anguish in times of grief and stress. I realize that I am bringing a Christian perspective to this issue, but I cannot see that there is any other response to questions that drive us back to God.

Think about contexts recently in which you asked "why?". What, if any, answers did you find?

4. My knowledge of whether there is a higher divine authority: Stanley Morton's quest

People use their retirement in many different ways. Stanley Morton set out on a specific quest. While still in his mid-fifties, he retired as a classics teacher to pursue research which had been impossible during his working years. He was well read and had a long-standing interest in comparative religion. The question of ultimate divine authority fascinated him, and especially because of his concerns about society's lack of acceptance of authority in general.

His search for literature led him to browse through many different categories on the Amazon website. In the popular Christian section he found books by people like Philip Yancey, who applies Christian principles to everyday life. In the early stages of his study, Stanley found one of Yancey's books especially relevant. He found the following remark particularly thought-provoking: "No society in history has attempted to live without a belief in the sacred, not until the modern West. Such a leap has consequences that we are only beginning to recognize. We now live in a state of confusion about the big questions that always engaged the human race, questions of meaning, purpose and reality."[43] Stanley agreed with Yancey about the state of confusion in the world, but he found few people either willing or equipped to engage in conversation on these questions. Yet he observed that when major world disasters occurred (such as September 11, 2001 or the Asian tsunami in December 2004), modern men and women immediately looked to a transcendent power. As evidence Stanley noted short-term boosts to attendance in places of worship, spontaneous calls for national prayer and appeals to a higher being for help for the leaders of the nations concerned. Perhaps, Stanley thought, many people do still have a basic belief – but most of the time it is replaced by poor substitutes that can be reached or touched. Or is this kind of response just superstitious, since these people appear to lack any belief system at other times?

Stanley had to admit that he was as guilty and inconsistent as the next person in this whole area. He was keen to find a more solid base for his own life, and the Christian view of a sovereign God appealed to him. Without the apparatus of theology, and with a slender knowledge of the Bible, he accepted some of the basic concepts underlying the Christian faith. From his observation of nature and the galaxies around us, he believed that the world was designed to perfection. He accepted that evil had marred that goodness and that it was rooted in men and women as a whole. But he was less sure of how this could be solved. He knew many good people who had faith, and equal numbers of good people

---

[43] Yancey, *Rumors*, p. 19.

who had no faith. Although he was depressed at times by the unbridled evil he saw all around him, he rejected the lack of hope such as that reflected in Macbeth's view of history: "A tale / Told by an idiot, full of sound and fury, / Signifying nothing."

Three years passed, while Stanley read and searched the major world religions for a solution for this problem of redemption for the world. He had heard and read many different versions of the truth about Christianity, and he had been unimpressed by some of the public divisions within the historic and contemporary church, but he had never read the primary source, the Bible. He was astonished to find that the Christian faith was in fact based on a massive rescue plan – the Creator God of the Bible, who offered himself as a sacrifice to redeem us, was at the same time the designer, creator and redeemer of the world. Stanley was not an emotional man, but he was profoundly moved when he found out that the motivation for all of this was love – and love for people like him. This was either fantastic or true – and if the latter, he had to believe. He urgently desired to know more.

Reflection:

"If your happiness comes from something that you deposit, drive, drink or digest, then face it – you are in prison, the prison of want." (Max Lucado)

From stumbling blocks to stepping stones

Events in our own lives and in those around us can cause us to think more deeply about what may be missing in our lives. Materialism (both in the form of prosperity and financial struggles) and suffering at a personal and global level can be stumbling blocks – yet, as we have seen above, they can also become stepping stones to faith. The examples below follow this transition from stumbling block to stepping stone.

Stumbling block: Injustice. Why do bad things happen to good people? Leslie Weatherhead, a Christian preacher and writer from the mid-twentieth century, helps us to understand how God's will can be a stepping stone rather than a hindrance.[44] He distinguished three ways of viewing the will of God, or what God allows to happen. The first he calls God's *intentional will*, namely his original design of perfection as we see it – for example, in the creation plan and in his ultimate intention to unite all things under Jesus Christ's rule. Second, there is God's *circumstantial will*. After sin came into the world through humankind's disobedience, God's will adapts to the evil conditions here – but his plans still go ahead. For example, the apostle Paul, falsely accused, spends much time in prison – but he still develops his theology there, and God's church building goes on. Finally there is God's *ultimate will*, wherein God can use any circumstance (however improbable) to fulfil his plans. How he does that remains a mystery. I rejoice in the knowledge that God's perspective and wisdom are far beyond what I can grasp or imagine. For me, the existence of God's sovereign will was a stepping stone to faith – and it has remained a bulwark throughout my life. I am thoroughly content to leave the ultimate outworking of his purposes to him.

Stumbling block: Invisible kingdom. While in some countries the Christian presence is much more evident than it is in others in terms of people, buildings and activity, Jesus spoke of his followers being almost a "secret force". He described the Christian community with images of things

---

[44] Leslie Weatherhead, *The Will of God* (Nashville: Abingdon, 1972).

that are small and inconsequential, like a seed that grows silently but effectively. He speaks of his "kingdom" as a mustard seed, as a pinch of yeast in bread, or as a sprinkling of salt on meat. Such pictures imply a consistent, powerful and positively directed set of activities. As C.S. Lewis says, "Enemy occupied territory – that's what this world is. Christianity is the story of how the rightful king has landed, you might say landed in disguise and is calling us all (as Christians) to take part in a great plan of sabotage."[45] Christianity is not a secret society, and each follower of Jesus is given a mission to fulfil quietly (and some more loudly) but effectively for God's glory. Seen from this angle, becoming a Christian is a stepping stone to a great adventure.

Stumbling block: God is far away. What kind of relationship can we possibly have with someone like God? The Bible clearly portrays God as a person with feelings and emotions, not as an impersonal force. Yet God is a spirit who is the creator and sustainer of all life. Reverence and friendship go hand-in-hand, as do love and fear. As with other personal relationships, there are good and bad times. Sometimes our communication with God is poor, we are disobedient and doubt clouds our relationship. We see some important figures in the Bible struggling with these issues in their relationship with God. For example, Moses argues with God over his role in leading the nation; Abraham takes things into his own hands when God takes too long fulfilling his promise; Jacob wrestles with him; and David breaks many of his commandments. David wrote extensively about his highs and lows in his relationship with God. During a time when his relationship with God was fractured because of his disobedience he wrote, "Create in me a pure heart, O God,

---

[45] Lewis, *Mere Christianity*, p. 47.

and renew a steadfast spirit within me."[46] He expresses his intense desire to live a God-centred life: "O God, you are my God, earnestly I seek you; my soul thirsts for you, my body longs for you, in a dry and weary land where there is no water."[47] God's desire is to have a close, personal relationship with us – and Jesus left heaven to make that possible. If you were to believe and accept this, it would solve a mystery and allow this biblical truth to become a vital stepping stone for you.

Stumbling block: God as Father. How can I see God as "Father" when my experience of my own father was so hurtful? The Houston family was a prime example of things not being exactly as they appeared to be. The image of external harmony that Bill Houston fought hard to maintain masked tensions with his wife, Margaret, and their daughter, Patricia. They had a lovely period home in a Cotswold village, a holiday cottage in the Loire and expensive cars. Patricia went to the best schools. Bill's successful and lucrative legal practice specialized in competition law, and his natural aggression and belligerent nature were assets in complex disputes involving major global companies. He had no tolerance for people of lesser intellect and few friends or social contacts outside legal circles.

Margaret no longer fitted into Bill's life. They were teenage sweethearts and very much in love throughout university, when Margaret worked long hours in several extra jobs to help finance Bill's studies. Bill used to proudly say, "I studied the law; Margaret made the money!" But now he denied both the fact and the sentiment behind it. Bill despised Margaret, criticized her in public, made fun of her "small-minded" interests and dress sense and much more. An expensive, messy and high-profile divorce was out of the question for

---

[46] Psalm 51:10.
[47] Psalm 63:1.

Bill – although Margaret had long been aware of his "discreet" affairs. Theirs was a marriage of convenience – Bill's.

It was in this unhappy home that Patricia grew up. Her father saw her as a clone of her mother and one of the props for her life. Seeing the close father-daughter relationships that her friends had made her envious and sad. "I can't do anything to please him, and he thinks of me as inferior in every way. The way he treats my mother is despicable. I can never forgive him." Patricia never saw any reason to celebrate Father's Day – to the contrary, she sometimes wept when she saw displays of cards for that event in the local supermarket.

Patricia left home to study biochemistry at a university hundreds of miles away. She quickly became good friends with her dorm mates, several of whom were Christians. One of the first events she attended was a supper, where they sang a song called "Abba, Father". As they walked home that evening, Patricia asked her friend Marion what this meant. Marion explained that it was one of the most remarkable concepts in the Bible. Jesus introduced his Father God to his followers and invited them to call him by the familiar family term of address – "daddy". This was a totally unacceptable idea to Patricia, and she rejected it outright. "I haven't called my father that for years because I have no affection for him, and the feeling's mutual. How can I talk about God like that?" Her bitterness towards her father was so deep-seated that it was a very long time before she was even able to say the Lord's Prayer. But gradually, as she began to see the dramatic difference between God's love for his children and everything she had ever experienced or imagined was possible, things changed. She came to know God as her Father in a special sense and she accepted Jesus Christ as her Saviour and Lord. Her massive stumbling block became the key building block for her life. "Who would have believed it?" she mused wistfully. "God is everything I ever dreamed a father could be – and more. I wonder if God will even give me the strength to forgive my own father?"

Food for thought:

If you haven't done so already, identify your major stumbling blocks. What is it that has prevented you from learning more about God? How might your stumbling block become a stepping stone to faith?

5

What's on offer?

"The whole human experience lies in this: that man may be able to bow down to the infinitely great." Fyodor Dostoevsky

"Jesus Christ is the same yesterday, today and forever." (Hebrews 13:8)

Outline

What does it look like? What is it like to actually live the Christian life?

What's in it for me? Unveils just four of the numerous treasures of the Christian life.

Defer, reject, negotiate, accept: People respond to this one offer God makes in many different ways.

What does it look like?

What's the deal? The direct, personal and biblical answer to this question is this: God will forgive the debt completely (your sins) and give you unlimited direct access to himself. Many other benefits ensue for your relationships and personal well-being as you pursue this new way of life. We'll discuss many of these benefits (the Bible calls them blessings) in this chapter.

As we think about what it looks like to live "the Christian life", we'll use the following definition: "the life of faith that God empowers his followers to live". The emphasis here is on the work that God does in us. He helps those who believe in him to understand and follow through on the conditions of discipleship, which we will examine in this and the following chapters. According to this definition, as we will see, mere church attendance or a vague subscription to Christian values – or anything equally worthy – does not constitute living the Christian life. We will also see that, although this is the life to which God wants Christians to aspire, it cannot be achieved without the power of the Spirit of God (as we saw in Chapter 3). The Christian bases his or her life on the principles that Jesus himself lived. While Christians around the world will differ in the interpretation of some beliefs and practices (many of which reflect diverse cultures and historical factors), our focus here is on the core principles that come directly from the teachings of Jesus.

The step of faith

The Christian life begins when we repent of the wrong things we've done, recognizing that Jesus died to pay the penalty for us, and we decide to follow the ways of Jesus instead of our own. In doing so we take on not only a new personal allegiance, but we also join a community with a worldwide reach. Jesus' death, its purpose and benefits, have attracted men and women since the day he died. But his death has also repelled others because of the shame, pain and horror with which it is associated – and also because it implicates them in his death, which they see as an unnecessary sacrifice for sin they didn't commit.

One of the first things that the new Christian notices is a new-found desire to please God. In our liberated age where authority is not generally respected, the image of servant and master is not popular. But in the freedom and grace of Jesus, Christians find joy in serving their Master. As C.S. Lewis observed, living a Christian life means "that every single act and feeling, every experience, whether pleasant or unpleasant, must be referred to God".[48] Far from being restrictive or demanding, this flows naturally as part of a close friendship with Jesus. We bring everything to him – joy and sorrow, strength and weakness, poverty and prosperity, blessing and suffering. He loves to hear from his disciples and they from him – the Bible describes this friendship between Jesus and the Christian as being "closer than a brother".

The person

The more I look, the more amazed I am by God's plan to bring salvation; by the fact that he sent his Son; by Jesus' character and qualities; and, perhaps above all, by his love and personal interest in me. The more I have come to know about God, the less worthy I feel that he designed this plan to include me. The thing that amazes me most about God is

[48] C.S. Lewis, *God in the Dock* (London: Harper Collins, 1971), p. 50.

his love. Jesus told a parable about a merchant who sold everything in order to buy the finest pearl he had ever seen. Nothing else was worth keeping once he saw this pearl. Each one of us is that pearl. God gave up everything, in the form of his own Son, to purchase our salvation. If you were to become a follower of Jesus you would find yourself drawn to his magnetism and feel a compulsion to respond.

The values

The values that the Bible sets out also attract me. Order and consistency pervade the book as it lays out the life that pleases God. The Bible is full of wisdom for family, social and personal conduct; its emphasis on love determines our attitudes towards ourselves and others; and it brings new perspectives on work, materialism and so much more. The Christian lives his or her life, the Bible teaches, as a response to the love of God. These values are part of the "package" of a life committed to Jesus. Christians can't opt in or out as they please. Embodying biblical values sets Christians apart from the rest of the world. Jesus described his followers as "a city set on a hill" and "a light to be seen by all people". It can be challenging to live out these values in all of the diverse circumstances of our lives. I have found this myself in church, at home, in the boardroom, in classes – and in everyday interactions being part of the human race! But the Holy Spirit is the power of God within us to be bold and strong in the face of opposition. God also gives us fellow believers to support and encourage one another along the way. There is an unparalleled richness, strength and love in Christian relationships.

The perspective

While the Christian's life on earth is full of opportunities and joys of many kinds, I have always been aware that I am a citizen of heaven and that this world is not my home. This has changed my perspective on everything – on what matters and what doesn't; on where I should spend time and money; on how I treat people and so on. The Christian looks to heaven as his or her promised eternal home – a place of joy, worship, rest and peace. Heaven will be free from the ravages of sin and suffering that mar this world – a "sin-free" zone that cannot be replicated anywhere else. (We will talk more about heaven in Chapter 8.) Seeing the world through a new prism makes an incredible difference.

The purpose

Jesus Christ brings me a new purpose. He calls for a life of worship and praise – not in the sense that we are in a permanent choir practice, but rather everything that we do gives God glory. For example, the Bible sees work as a form of service in which Christians engage. Similarly, we are to show the love of God to others on a daily basis and offer all of our resources to his service. Living a Christian life is a full-time job – and totally integrated with all other aspects of life. I have always found pursuing God's purpose in my life to be full of joy and blessing – but never simple, nor without challenges and troubles. At times, living the Christian life has been nothing short of a struggle as other priorities crush in on me. But I have never failed to experience God's strength and provision, even in the most trying of circumstances.

Relationship restored

"Relationship" with God? Yes, the Bible tells us that God created each one of us to relate closely to him – but the disobedience of sin ruptured that relationship. C.S. Lewis explains that need within us for a relationship with our creator: "Man's efforts to be like gods can never succeed. God made us: invented us as man invented an engine. A car is made to run on petrol, and it would not run properly on anything else. Now God designed the human machine to run on Himself. He Himself is the fuel our spirits were designed to burn, or the food our spirits were designed to feed on. There is no other."[49] God's master plan is to restore that relationship through the work of Jesus Christ on the cross. That restoration is the essential foundation for living the Christian life. Without it we may be moral reformers, good people or sympathetic listeners – but no more. "Your real, new self will not come along as you are looking for it. It will come when you are looking for Him [Christ]".[50]

Behaviour altered

The life lived for Jesus is markedly different from the life that is not. Although none of God's commands are onerous, we do not behave the same way if God is directing our thoughts, words and actions. The apostle Paul illustrates the extremes of this. He contrasts negative behaviour (such as sexual immorality, envy, hatred and jealousy), which is to be shunned by those who follow God's will, with the great virtues of love, joy, patience, peace and so on that we saw

---

[49] Lewis, *Mere Christianity*, p. 50.
[50] Lewis, *Mere Christianity*, p. 188.

earlier.[51] How would you handle relationships and situations differently if you were applying these virtues where you work and live? However welcome these are in principle, it is difficult to apply them with consistency. Indeed, Jesus tells us that we are to expect opposition – just as he himself did. The "scars" that result are (metaphorically or literally) marks of identification for every disciple of Jesus.

Progress recorded

The Christian life is one of growth. The Bible explains this development through the natural life cycle, starting with childhood. Jesus, with a child standing before him, faced questions from ambitious followers about who would be greatest in his kingdom. He told them, "I tell you the truth, unless you change and become like little children, you will never enter the kingdom of heaven".[52] Irrespective of chronological age, education or experience, we all begin in the faith as children – trusting, believing and welcoming the gift. In some senses, "faith" will always be childlike, but there is a difference between that simple trust and a childish faith that looks for magic solutions.

In the more mature interactions of adulthood we build on relationships by spending time together discussing issues in greater depth, planning joint activities and so on. The Bible often pictures the Christian training for the race of life. He or she also becomes increasingly aware of the implications of the fact that the Spirit of God lives within, as he or she strives for purity in thought and deed. Another picture of adulthood is the disciple as an ambassador for Jesus, representing him here on earth. The Christian life is one of action.

---

[51] Galatians 5:22–23.

[52] Matthew 18:3.

In the natural progression of Christian maturity, "parenthood" follows. All maturing Christians have an obligation to nurture and encourage others to follow Jesus, as well as to serve others – regardless of what they believe. Christians take being a good citizen of earth as seriously as being a citizen of heaven. Following Jesus means following his example of service and love. "This is how we know what love is: Jesus Christ laid down his life for us. And we ought to lay down our lives for one another."[53] Part of growing in maturity also involves accountability. As all people mature and take on extra responsibilities in life in general, they need to give an account of their actions to different people. Such a consciousness also develops in Christians. As we exercise free will and make personal choices, we also need to take seriously Jesus' examples of testing. How have we used the resources we've been allocated? What is the motivation behind our behaviour?

Invitation unheeded?

But why does the Christian life not appeal to many people in Western societies? I have struggled with this question for many years, in conversations with friends and colleagues. I don't assume that, because I find Jesus Christ attractive as the foundation for my life, you will also. Nothing would give me more pleasure than if you did, but I can only give you the facts, offer guidance from my own experience, and make some recommendations. I have no power to influence your choice.

Many people have concluded that there is too much that is negative and restrictive about Christianity as a lifestyle. Some of these conclusions are based on personal experience,

---

[53] 1 John 3:16.

some on their (understandably) negative interpretation of some of church history and the abuse of religion. Equally, however, many Christians are not actively living and proclaiming the joys and blessings of the Christian life. Others don't see how being a Christian would "add value" to their lives. I find, however, that this remark is not usually based on much thought and underestimates or belittles the "value" of the spiritual. For example, I would say that having peace, forgiveness and eternal security are transformational by any standards – but not all see it that way.

In contemporary Western society, many of us can live successful and comfortable lives without reference to God. There are so many other attractions, so many other things and relationships to which we can devote our time and energy – and they become, in fact, our gods. Money and materialism are chief among them, success and career progression follow close behind. We also have a perhaps unprecedented confidence in our own ability to control our environment. And Christianity's counter-cultural message might mean relinquishing some of that control – over our own behaviour and over that of others. While some people simply have been blinded by the trappings of a comfortable life, there are also those who have spent many years and much effort eluding God's voice, the encouragement of others and their own consciences. The greatest barrier to Christianity in Western society, perhaps, is the fact that few people take time out to think about eternity. "Quality time" – for family, business, or leisure – is a common topic of conversation in our "time starved" generation. But who thinks about spending quality time with God?

A great many people, too, reject the idea of being different from their peers and resist such a radical change. Despite the fact that we are all living through a period of unprecedented change, this change seems a step too far. There is an old prayer that says, "Lord, help me to change, but not too much, and not too soon". Each of us also carries an element of pride – pride that denies the need to acknowledge sin, or confess it, or accept that something fundamental has gone wrong in our lives and needs to be fixed.

While we have begun to scratch the surface of the Christian life here, we continue the discussion in Chapter 6, where we look at the experiences of those who find Jesus, and in Chapter 8, where we think about choosing spiritual goals for life.

> **Reflection:**
>
> What seems attractive to you about the Christian life or the idea of having faith in Jesus? What are your fears or reservations about following Jesus? If you have a Christian friend or colleague, talk with him or her about these questions and concerns.

What's in it for me?

The Christian life is so full of treasures and rich reward, it's impossible to do justice to them all. What follows, then, are four truths that have recently been very poignant for me and may prove to be helpful to you at this stage in your search.

First, it's a miracle. Some people say that the idea that Jesus performed miracles while he was on earth is a stumbling block to the rational minds of modern men and women. This line of argument suggests that if Christianity were somehow freed from its miraculous elements, it might help belief. C.S. Lewis once responded forcefully to such a proposition by saying that you might well do this to other religions without changing their fundamentals ". . . but you cannot possibly do that with Christianity, because the Christian story is precisely the story of one grand miracle, the Christian assertion being that what is behind all space and time, what is uncreated, eternal, came into nature, into human nature, descended into His own universe, and rose again, bringing nature up with Him . . . if you take that away, there is nothing specifically left".[54] Lewis accurately describes this as "The Grand Miracle". He is right. And you and I can be part of it. As Albert Einstein observed, "There are two ways to live your life. One is though nothing is a miracle. The other is though everything is a miracle".

Second, God lives in me. In spite of its wide usage, the term "Christian" is not the word the Bible most commonly uses to describe a follower of Jesus Christ. Instead, the Bible speaks of something more intimate and more personal, emphasizing what God has made possible – namely, a new relationship which involves Jesus Christ living within us. Many biblical passages bring out this remarkable principle. The first one is part of Paul's prayer for the church in Ephesus. "I pray that out of his glorious riches he may strengthen you with power through his Spirit in your inner being, so that Christ *may dwell in your hearts* through faith. And I pray that you, being rooted and established in love, may have power, together with all the saints, to grasp how wide and long and high and deep is the love of Christ, and to know this love that surpasses knowledge – that you may be filled to the measure of all the fulness of God."[55] The two-way nature of this relationship emerges in a passage such as this one: "Those who obey his commands *live in him, and he in them*. And this is how we know that he lives in us: We know

[54] Lewis, *God in the Dock*, p. 56.

[55] Ephesians 3:16–19 (italics mine).

it by the Spirit he gave us."[56] Throughout the New Testament we see this precondition of obedience, and the confirmation of God's presence with us is the fruit of the Spirit, the work of the Spirit we discussed in Chapter 3. We see the fruit of the Spirit in every aspect of our lives – our thoughts, speech, actions, decisions, lifestyle and so much more.

Third, God makes me a new person. I was struck recently by C.S. Lewis' comparisons between the transformations that take place in nature and the spiritual transformation that God makes possible through Jesus.[57] He suggests that no one could have predicted that the "next step" for humankind would come through the cross of Jesus Christ. This transformation went in a completely new direction – indeed, it was a change from being creatures of God to children of God. This change does not arise out of a natural process but comes into nature from the outside. Among the other differences is the fact that we can refuse the offer of this transformation (as many do!). Jesus Christ is the first example of this "new person" – indeed, he is the New Man. Lewis also observes that this step for humankind has occurred at a relatively fast pace, given the rapid diffusion of Christianity over the past two thousand years. In the West, people often claim that the church is dying. But it remains very much alive and is expanding in new places. As Lewis puts it, the "New Man" rose again and keeps on rising again in us. This is a wonderfully optimistic perspective from which to view my faith, and it fills me with hope and gives me a surge of new life and renewed purpose even as I write it now. These "new people" are everywhere – irregardless of all the other gender, cultural and social features that separate people. They are all different, yet he made them all.

---

[56] 1 John 3:24 (italics mine).

[57] Lewis, *Mere Christianity*, pp. 181–91.

Fourth, and perhaps unexpectedly, I count the fact that God calls for sacrifice among the treasures of God's offer. Part of our natural response to God's sacrifice on our behalf is to serve him with the resources that he has give us, turning everything over to his control.[58] One of the classical biblical statements on this comes from Paul. "Therefore, I urge you, brothers and sisters, in view of God's mercy, to offer your bodies as living sacrifices, holy and pleasing to God – this is your spiritual act of worship."[59] What Christians give is always in response to God's initial gift – it's a reciprocal, almost reflex, action, but it is never ill-considered. In the pressures of life this is not always easy, but it is pivotal and lies right at the core of what being "in Jesus" involves. The "sacrifice" takes many forms – our praise, worship and thanksgiving to God; our time and resources spent serving others; prayer; bending our wills to his in obedience; gifts and good deeds given in his name, and so on. In all of these things we both give and gain.

Reflection:

Take a few minutes to reflect on one of the following wise sayings: "The life of every man is a diary in which he means to write one story, and writes another." (J.M. Barrie) Have you been writing the story that you wanted to write? If not, what parts of the planned narrative have not turned out as you thought they would?

"The best use of life is to spend it on something that outlasts life." (William James) Will you spend your life on something that outlasts life itself? If so, how?

---

[58] For more detailed treatment of these issues see my *Whose Life?* trilogy.

[59] Romans 12:1.

Defer, reject, negotiate, accept

Let's think about God's offer from a completely different perspective for a moment. Commercial language, with which we are all familiar, helps us to draw some parallels in terms of how we perceive God's offer of mercy and grace.

Always on offer

That's the way Jason looked at the Christian gospel – and he was correct, up to a point. There were plenty of churches, loads of websites and books and literature everywhere. He was fairly interested in all of this, but his philosophy was simple. "There's no rush. I'm twenty-eight and I want to enjoy my youth. I'll think seriously about God's offer when I'm older and more settled. Then I'll be able to make a more mature decision anyway." Unfortunately, Jason never had that chance. Jason was a plant engineer with an international construction company. While on a site visit in Germany, he was killed while inspecting a bucket on a massive drag line in an open cast coal mine on the Ruhr. Jason knew a lot about the "offer", he was interested in amassing information about it and he felt its appeal – but he seems to have failed to accept it.

Offer rejected

Nigel was a cynic to his fingertips and criticized anyone who suggested that there was more to life than the "here and now". A well-educated man and an expert in artificial intelligence, he specialized in testing all ideas to destruction. He was a fierce debater, but not a very sociable person. In general, he viewed religious beliefs as not being worthy of his cerebral faculties. The research institute in which he was employed had many equally able scholars – so Nigel was never short of sparring partners when it came to mental puzzles and mind games. Marina was one such colleague, a microbiologist of Greek origin and of international repute. She had an outstanding mind and an appetite to challenge cynics. She was also a Christian, and this puzzled Nigel. But it did not stir his interest enough to want to share her faith. In fact, Nigel was quite clear that he wanted nothing to do with it. "Marina, I want you to explain to me how I can get all of these ideas of 'God' out of my head. I'm just not interested, but I keep stumbling upon issues that I find disturbing, like ultimate justice and accountability – and does something happen after this life? I just want to live my own life now." Marina had many subsequent conversations with Nigel, but she never told Nigel how to get God out of his mind. No Christian would want to do that – even if she could.

Negotiating a discount

Kenneth loved a bargain. He prided himself that he never paid the full price for anything. "Price is a point on a spectrum; the point you finally arrive at depends on how tough a negotiator you are. I like nothing better than a good battle over a deal." The trouble was, Kenneth thought you could apply this philosophy to everything. For example, he had several failed relationships because, when they became serious, he wanted prenuptial agreements to make sure that any future failure would not lead to financial loss. Kenneth had a few tenuous church connections because he liked modern music and was fond of singing. He sometimes attended church concerts with his neighbours, Andy and Janette Murphy. After one of these events he had coffee in their home. The conversation went something like this.

"Andy," Kenneth said, "I've been thinking about your God and his terms. I like the idea of being a more content and better person, and I like your friends, but I'm not really into theology. If I didn't have to follow all of the biblical commandments, and love *everybody*, I think I could pretty much buy into Christianity. Oh, and I don't really like the idea of turning the other cheek when someone offends me, either. What do you think? Could I make a deal, as they say, with God so we'd both be happy?" Andy was astonished. "Sorry, Kenneth. God doesn't work that way. His is an offer of complete forgiveness and he doesn't negotiate with anybody. Dealing with him is a purely spiritual transaction, I'm afraid, and it's all or nothing."

Accepting the offer

Unlike Kenneth, Marcia realized that God's offer was free. She knew that what she had to do was to come to terms with his generosity. Marcia had low self-esteem for several reasons. Her siblings were much brighter than she ever was at school, and she disappointed her parents in every career goal they set for her. Their expectations diminished – from a career in medicine as a doctor, to a nurse, and then to a care worker. Both of her parents blamed her for a lack of concentration and effort. Her brother and sister both sympathized with Marcia. "Dad, you're being unreasonable. Just because you haven't achieved all of your goals in life, you can't dump your unfulfilled ambitions on Marcia." There was more friction in the Sheringham home over this matter than about anything else. The care home where Marcia worked was indeed a "home from home" for her. It was organized by a Christian housing association, and she loved the work. Her heart lay in caring for the disadvantaged young people who lived there. Through talking with Christians who worked with her, gradually Marcia became very interested in God's offer. It was so full, so unconditional, and so complete – so she took it without reservation. God's love transformed her as it gave her new confidence and joy, and even a new love for, and understanding of, her parents.

Food for thought:

"The Christian ideal has not been tried and found wanting, it has been found difficult and left untried." (G.K. Chesterton)

How do you respond to God's offer?

6

What's the journey like?

"And what is achieved through the cross is no merely external change of legal status, since those who see God's love there, and are united to Christ by his Spirit, become radically transformed in outlook and character."
(John Stott)[60]

"For he has rescued us from the dominion of darkness and brought us into the kingdom of the Son he loves." (Colossians 1:13)

Outline

Introduction: Answers some of the questions that people considering Christianity commonly ask and considers the role of faith, fear and promises in a Christian's life.

Tests of faith: Faith is always tested. The lives of Abraham, Elijah and Moses, as well as Judas and Cain, teach us about the consequences of the choices we make when God tests us.

Doubts: All of us doubt at one time or another. How did Jesus treat people with honest doubts?

Life stories: The experiences of three different people illustrate the kinds of challenges and opportunities new Christians face as they begin their journeys of faith.

---

[60] Stott, *Cross*, p. 159.

Introduction

This chapter answers some basic questions about what it's like to be a Christian. For example, "If I do find Jesus, what will it be like to be a new Christian?" "How would serving Jesus change my life?" "Is there any guarantee I'll have a better, healthier or wealthier life?" "What can I do to make sure that all these promises from God that Christians tell me about actually are fulfilled?"

No matter how seasoned a traveller you may be, all journeys require some preparation. All of the experiences you have had, skills you have acquired and difficulties you have faced have already prepared you for what lies ahead in your life. God gives the new Christian many other resources, including the Bible and the Holy Spirit. We also have the amazing reassurance that Jesus Christ travelled through the twists and turns of this life before us. Mysterious though it sounds, Christians know that they travel with the most experienced traveller in the universe.

Spiritual transformation, both internal and external, is an essential part of this journey. All of us need all the help we can get – from God and from other Christians – as we embark on this journey. Fyodor Dostoevsky observed the human need for finding our "formula", or our pattern and meaning. "Every ant knows the formula of its ant-hill, every bee knows the formula of its beehive. They know it in their own way, not in our way. Only humankind does not know its formula." As we saw in Chapter 4, following Jesus Christ (and entrusting our lives to him) leads us back to God's original formula for the human race. Our challenge is to apply this pattern to our daily lives.

Anticipating the journey

Three insights into the nature of this journey stand out as being particularly helpful. These three – applying faith, recognizing fear and being certain of God's promises – address real areas of concern in which we often need reassurance.

Applying faith. Any journey requires some measure of faith – from faith that the aeroplane will fly or the car will start, to faith that no accidents will occur, that colleagues or friends will meet you at your destination, that the hotel will actually have your reservation and so on. The "what ifs" are endless. But these are so routine to us that we rarely give them a second thought. The role of faith in the Christian journey is quite different. The Christian journeying through this world is constantly aware of his or her need for faith. Being a Christian means doing things, going in certain directions and making choices that can only be accomplished in the strength of faith. As the Bible tells us, "Now faith is being sure of what we hope for and certain of what we do not see."[61] This definition of faith in the New Testament book of Hebrews introduces a series of life journeys of Old Testament believers who relied upon their faith. For example, because of Abel's faith he knew what kind of sacrifice would please God. In the same way, Christians today need to know God in order to know how to use our talents to best serve him. Abraham needed faith to emigrate to a country hundreds of miles away which he had never visited. Moses' faith enabled him to suffer slavery and eventually to lead his people through many dangers to freedom. Faith involves taking risks and facing uncertainty. But faith is never blind, and Christians do not do this alone.

---

[61] Hebrews 11:1.

Recognizing fear. The most common biblical injunction to all followers is "Fear not". No matter how confident, self-assured and independent we are, there are times when we will be afraid. The fears Christians face may not be very different from those encountered in the normal course of life – for example, uncertainties over health, family, security and employment. New fears may revolve around how to implement Christian principles, how to share your faith with our friends, family and colleagues, or how to confront opposition to your faith. While the Bible is clear that Christians do face challenges, it is also clear that God equips us and that we can have great confidence. We often gain this confidence by having a glimpse of the bigger picture, from God's perspective. For example, the Christian's goal is to bring glory and praise to God, even honouring God by the way he or she copes with adversity. For example, Jesus explained the illness of a blind man when he said, "but this happened so that the work of God might be displayed in his life".[62] As I know from personal experience of serious illness, the Christian can only experience peace and the absence of fear by constantly asking for God's perspective. I can also assure you that this is exactly what God has given me, on many occasions. The 1945 Rodgers and Hammerstein Broadway musical "Carousel" included the memorable song "You'll Never Walk Alone". The Christian experiences this truth in an entirely new, and eternal, dimension.

Remembering God's promises. The Bible often speaks of God's blessings for his people in grand and glorious terms: for example, "Praise be to the God and Father of our Lord Jesus Christ, who has blessed us in the heavenly realms

---

[62] John 9:3.

with every spiritual blessing in Christ."[63] It's important to remember that the most important blessings for the Christian journey are "spiritual" ones. Our new relationship with God is a spiritual one, and so our spirit needs to be strengthened by God at every turn. Christians look for these blessings – and find them – in discovering strength to face new challenges they once would have thought impossible; in being able to forgive what might once have seemed unforgivable; in finding words to say when, humanly speaking, there seem to be no words; in new insights and courage and peace that pass human understanding. God may also add other, more "tangible" blessings to the Christian's life – often in ways that might seem unimaginable now. While these blessings are very real, not all Christians enjoy them in each and every situation in which they find themselves. Practical and personal challenges such as poverty, persecution and depression can cause great struggles and battles. In such situations, the following is one of my favourite promises because it assures not just any victory, but the victorious conquering Jesus Christ: "But thanks be to God, who always leads us in triumphal procession in Christ and through us spreads everywhere the fragrance of the knowledge of him."[64] God wants every Christian's journey to have this glorious and joyful end. The picture is of a conquering hero, leading a grand, triumphal procession in the company of all who have contributed to his victory, and leaving a sweet fragrance that attracts others as they watch the procession. In Jesus' case, all of us were among the enemies of the victor; Christians, having responded to his victory on the cross, are now part of his triumphal procession.

---

[63] Ephesians 1:3.
[64] 2 Corinthians 2:14.

Tests of faith

The Bible is remarkable for its honesty in describing the lives of the men and women recorded in biblical history. While history books are famed for glamorizing and reinterpreting facts and events to show leading figures, and even countries and governments, in the best possible light, not so the Bible. Below are a few brief portraits of some real people who faced major tests of their faith. Some came through; others failed. Those who remained strong in the faith have been examples to us for countless generations.

Passing the test

Abraham at Mount Moriah. After God promises Abraham that he will found a nation, God asks him to take his only and much loved son, Isaac, to Mount Moriah as a sacrifice. Abraham does as God asks, and we can only imagine his mental turmoil. God stops Abraham from sacrificing his son and commends him for his fear of the Lord, as shown in his willingness to obey him.[65] God blesses Abraham greatly, fulfilling all of his promises to him and to his descendants

Elijah in a desert. Elijah's test comes shortly after his greatest triumph. God had agreed to Elijah's request to show his awesome power to destroy heathen gods and their worshippers. Seeing the consequences of this event, the powerful Jezebel predicts Elijah's death and her forces pursue him so that he is forced to flee to the desert. Elijah lies in the desert, a broken and disillusioned man. God snaps him out of his deep depression by giving him personal assurances of support and a clear direction for his future

---

[65] Genesis 22.

work. Elijah has faith in God's promises and continues to serve him powerfully and wholeheartedly.[66]

Moses at the burning bush. God grooms Moses for many years to lead his people out of Egypt and finally reveals his plan to Moses at this burning bush. In spite of a clear call from God, Moses vigorously protests that this is not a job for which he is naturally qualified. Moses faces God's anger and pleads that he ask someone else to do it. With his brother Aaron's help, Moses takes the job on and succeeds in leading his people out of Egypt.[67]

Failing the test

Judas and the treasure. One of Jesus' team of twelve disciples, Judas Iscariot finds that his desire for money overrides his loyalty. Judas' test calls him to betray his master, and he fails it miserably. Judas is a witness to the teaching and miracles of Jesus, in the inner circle, yet his life ends in tragic failure and suicide.[68]

Cain and the murder. In dispute with God over the acceptability of his sacrificial offering, Cain looks for an outlet for his anger. He finds it close to home in his brother, for Cain perceives that God had treated Abel more favourably. So Cain murders Abel and lies to God about his whereabouts.[69]

---

[66] 1 Kings 19.
[67] Exodus 3 and 4.
[68] Mark 14.
[69] Genesis 4.

Doubts

Even Christians are sometimes unsure about wholly
believing (or understanding) certain biblical truths. All of us
harbour some sort of doubts about faith or facts. A degree of
mystery surrounds all of the foundational truths of the
Christian faith – for example, the victory of the cross, the
resurrection of Jesus and the power of the Spirit. The Bible
is a historical document, but it also records truths that
human beings can never "prove" empirically. That's where the
faith comes in. In taking their step of faith, Christians need
to acknowledge the reality of opposition. Satan, or the devil,
is real and it is his business to attack the Christian's
confidence in Jesus; to cause us to question why Christianity
is unique; to create confusion about God's guidance; to fuel
fears that God will not take care of our future; to convince
us that the biblical promises are not true, and so on.
Christians need to see this opposition for what it is –
guerrilla-like tactics designed to divert us from the way
ahead.

In all of this, I take encouragement from the gentle way
Jesus treated doubters and from the patience he
demonstrated in his interactions with many of them. Let's
look at two examples. John the Baptist came to announce
the coming of Jesus Christ. But John, who was in prison at
the time, heard of Jesus' work and had doubts about who he
was. John sent his disciples to Jesus to clarify the situation.
Given the divinely-ordained interlinking of their births and
family connections, John must surely have had ample
evidence to convince him who Jesus was. It would have been
understandable had Jesus been irritated by this questioning
and lack of belief, but he showed no sign of that. On the
contrary, he tells the messengers to take back details of his
work to John and he speaks in glowing terms about John

and his ministry.[70] Then there is Thomas, the disciple who had difficulty believing that the resurrection had actually happened because he had not seen Jesus with his own eyes. He boldly declared that unless he saw the nail marks, put his finger in the place where the nails were, and put his hand into his side, he would not believe. There was a measure of aggression in his tone, but a week later his desire was fulfilled. Jesus tells him to stop doubting and believe, and his gentle rebuke evokes two responses. The first is from Thomas, who cries out, "My Lord and My God!"[71] The second is for us – Jesus declares his blessing on all those who have not seen and yet have believed.

Christians are called to give honest answers to honest questions. And sometimes the hard questions come down to an answer that involves faith. While God has given us minds as well as hearts, and wants us to use the intellect he's given us, there is no ultimate logical formula to prove who God is or what he has done. Cold intellectual inquiry alone will never bring you, or anyone else, into a relationship with the living God. Jesus advised his followers to be wary of those who engaged in intellectual trickery to trip up the weak and unwary.

Life stories

The following stories explore the early, and very different, experiences of three new Christians and the reactions of those around them to their new-found faith and lifestyle changes. All three share excitement and challenge during the early days of their Christian journeys. We can learn from and be encouraged by all of them as we continue to think about what the Christian life, or journey, looks like.

---

[70] Matthew 11.
[71] John 20:28.

1. Marty's mission

Marty Piper was Professor of Philosophy of Religion at a respected university. He was a leading scholar in his field and an excellent teacher who received such great course reviews from his students that his classes were usually oversubscribed. He was not without his flaws, one of which was that, while he championed debate on all religious matters, he was highly opinionated about some topics. Maybe this was because Marty was a convinced and rather militant atheist. Not only did he promote his own views about God with vigour, however, but he also quickly identified any signs of Christian interest in his graduate students and sought to destroy it by force of argument and personality. (He took a similar approach to all faiths founded on a supreme divine authority.) While Marty experienced mixed success in this "mission", he did a lot of damage and generated much uncertainty. Mari and Harry, two of Marty's students from recent years, had very different experiences under his tutelage.

Mari Spence was in her early thirties and had recently come to Christian faith. Mari had grown up in a broken home and had spent much of her life with relatives or in foster homes. By age seventeen she had drifted into prostitution. On her nineteenth birthday, late at night in a city bus station, she ran into her Aunt Anna. Mari hadn't had any contact with Anna for years, but they chatted and Anna invited Mari back to her home to stay for a few days. Mari found it difficult to adjust to a home and to genuine, unconditional kindness. Anna was loving, but direct. "You're ruining your life, Mari. I want to help you without running your life." After several difficult months, during which Anna was very patient, Mari decided to go to college. Her life was not totally in order, but she now funded her somewhat more manageable alcohol and drug addictions by working part-time stocking shelves in a supermarket. The company had a forward-thinking substance abuse policy and quickly identified her problem. Mari responded to their offer of help with enthusiasm – hence the beginning of a turning point in her life. She began to realize that there were options available to her, for education and lifestyle choices, and she wanted to make these changes. She knew that the journey would be difficult, but her aunt was a great support. Her experience at the local addiction centre proved to be life-changing in every sense, and it was through Christian volunteers there that she came to faith.

Three years later, she was a graduate student in one of Marty Piper's classes. Far from being vulnerable to his persistent and vigorous critique of her faith, Mari was perceptive enough to see through her professor. "Marty, I'm a Christian – even though I still have doubts and questions at times and am not adept at defending the faith in argument. I admire your skill with concepts and your facility with language – but I need more than that. I don't know how exactly, but Jesus has rescued me and I'm not going to let him go." Marty was flustered and rather taken aback – but he could not deny her sincerity, nor could he rob her of her experience. It made him think about his cynicism – and the incongruity in his own life. He knew he was good with words, but they didn't translate into actions or the kind of contentment and peace he saw in Christians like Mari.

Another of Marty's students was Harry Preston. Harry was in his mid-twenties and came from a very religious family. Harry's father, Peter, was a Baptist pastor. Harry had drifted into Christian faith almost by default – through a combination of compliance and parental pressure. Peter encouraged Harry to take classes with Marty Piper at his alma mater, believing his son to be sufficiently grounded in his faith to stand up to such challenges. But he wasn't. In fact, under Marty's influence Harry started to go back through his life to identify all of the repressive influences under which he had grown up and he became very angry with his parents, and especially with his father. Harry's criticisms shook his family to the core. Peter wondered how he had managed to get things so wrong. He reflected about how his church duties had dominated his time and he felt that he really did not know his son very well.

For years, Harry was one of Marty's "trophies". His faith had melted away – and his life had also lost direction. The problems Harry experienced were of no interest to Marty, who felt only that he had done his duty by releasing Harry from the shackles of mythology so that his mind was now open to receive new ideas as they came along. Marty couldn't have cared less about the consequences in Harry's life in terms of his relationships and choices. Harry went through the pain of a failed marriage and continued to struggle for many years to find out who he was. He was a prodigal – separated from God, his heavenly Father, and from his earthly father. It wasn't until Harry was in his forties that he reconciled with Peter, and not until he was in his fifties, when a serious illness threatened, that he reconnected with God.

Marty took his atheism to the grave at the age of fifty-three. He had only just begun to see that there was more to life than a powerful intellect. And he had begun to see, too, the scars left by what he had taken pleasure in destroying.

2. Benjamin's passage

When Benjamin decided in his late twenties to convert from his Jewish faith to Christianity, he knew this would change his life completely. He also knew that the way ahead would be tough. While his family members were liberal in their Jewish practice, they celebrated the traditional festivals with enthusiasm and held to the traditional values and Jewish identity with tenacity. Family was everything – and no one in this family had ever suggested moving from the faith. Their roots could be traced to Saint Petersburg as far back as the eighteenth century. His family regarded Benjamin's Christianity as an insult to them and to the entire community. The leaders in the synagogue were stunned. It would have been easier for them to come to terms with his absence or passive compliance with Judaism than his conversion to Christianity. He had shown such promise in his studies of the Torah and the Hebrew language in his teenage years. Rabbi Jacob said, "What a disappointment! I wonder how we could have nurtured him better and prevented this?" The reality was, he couldn't have. The genesis of Benjamin's conversion lay in his Old Testament studies, which raised questions in his mind about what God was like and how he should personally relate to him.

When he went to college, Benjamin looked in vain for a Jewish study group among the vast array of student organizations. There was no such group. Given that he was a spiritually aware person, he looked in at Islamic, Hindi and Christian groups. Thinking that he could find some answers to his biblical questions, he decided to attend the latter. He had contemplated the powerful yet harsh image of Jahweh in the books of Moses. He saw that people like David and Jeremiah had ups and downs in their relationships with God, but he noted that these relationships were based on worship, not friendship. He knew the history that, in spite of God's awesome demonstrations of power in their presence, the nation of Israel did not consistently love or obey him. He wanted to know why. Who was this God?

Benjamin's father, David, watched these developments in his son with interest and some trepidation. Though what Benjamin had decided to pursue was unusual, visible and formal, he hoped that it might be a passing phase. He faced some criticism from his more orthodox friends for his lack of action, and he quietly worked out a plan of action to implement if Benjamin's behaviour did not change.

In this college Christian fellowship group, Benjamin discovered the truth about Jesus the Messiah. He had never read the New Testament and had known nothing about Jesus being God's Son. Benjamin was amazed by Jesus' humility in entering this world; by his care for the poor and needy; by the familiarity of the language that he taught his disciples to use to address God (such intimate terms for God were unthinkable to a devout Jew). He was moved by the courage that Jesus displayed as he set aside his glory to come to earth, and he was shocked by the shame and curse of the cross. All of this, and so much more, burned in his mind and soul. For the first time he saw the Bible as a unified whole – built around the good news of Jesus Christ. He had choices to make – he knew it would be difficult with his family, but there was no question in his mind. Jesus Christ had died to be his saviour, and he passionately believed that. It had taken almost six years to get to this point, but his "conversion" was complete and he did not attempt to hide it from his family. His father accepted the reality and finality of these events.

His father felt he had no choice, then, but to implement the sanctions he had planned. "I'm withdrawing my offer of a partnership in the family property company," his father announced. "You will not feature in my final will and testament. And you can't stay here, but I will give you enough to buy a small flat." None of this surprised Benjamin, and he accepted it as part of the cost of discipleship. He was sad that his father was focusing on money – the passion of his father's life. He knew that there would be more costs to come, but he kept them in the perspective of what Jesus did on the cross for him and he truly felt his "losses" were nothing. He had found Jesus, his long search had come to an end. He looked forward to putting his intelligence and skills to work for God.

His mother Sarah's heart was broken, and Benjamin prayed that his family would follow him to Christian faith. They never did, but he worked hard to keep the strained relationships alive. God had shown all the initiative to rebuild relationships with humankind, and he vowed that he would follow that example. He experienced many hurtful rebuffs, but he found many supportive Christian friends and formed a small group with other Jewish converts. This group was invaluable. They were not only able to help each other within the group, but its members also helped many others to understand the pressures they had faced from their own flesh and blood.

Benjamin loved the Bible, and one of his favourite verses from the Psalms of David tied together the teachings of his youth and the new foundations for his Christian faith. "Not to us, O LORD, not to us but to your name be the glory, because of your love and faithfulness."[72]

3. Mark's morality

The close comradeship among Mark St. John's colleagues extended to all aspects of social and family life. Mark had been a firefighter based in a large city-centre station for

---

[72] Psalm 115:1.

fifteen years. The job was dangerous and required ongoing specialist training in controlling and preventing fires. His section fought hazardous fires in hospitals, in factories producing hazardous substances, in tall office blocks, in major educational establishments and in bonded warehouses. He and his colleagues also had to attend to many serious accidents on the city's motorways. Teamwork and close bonding were essential in the firefighter teams. Great care was taken to ensure compatibility among team members and monitor any changes in the "chemistry" between them.

Mark loved his work and his wife, Annette, fully supported him in it. She was very much a part of the social networks that formed around the station. There was, however, one spin-off from Mark's job that had bothered him for years – the corruption associated with some of the salvage work which followed fire outbreaks in premises such as retail warehouses and department and electrical goods stores. It was an unspoken assumption among the team members that certain saleable items were "made available", or taken as a reward, for services. Not all of it was illegal, and some was done with the full knowledge of the owners, but much of this behaviour was on the wrong side of the law and a long-standing cause of concern for the insurers.

What had been a minor discomfort to Mark for many years became a major crisis when he became a Christian at age thirty-five. His family had benefited from some of these goods when the budget was tight and the financial needs of a growing family rose every month. Several of their large kitchen appliances and the children's bicycles had come from these sources. Mark, but not Annette, had been exploring Christianity for several years. He had quietly been reading a New Testament for the past two years, at first with little interaction with Christians. He had discovered the book in an old briefcase and then learned of its power to change lives when he met an old drinking mate at a rugby game. "Mark, I've never had the chance to share my faith with you and tell you how my life has been totally transformed," Harold told him. Harold shared his dramatic story of rescue from alcohol addiction when he was on the verge of taking his own life. Mark found this hard to believe at first, since he had always regarded Harold, a medical professional, as a solid citizen. But things are not always as they seem. As he continued to meet and discuss his spiritual search with Harold, Mark learned just how infectious Harold's faith was. Mark, who had always denied sin, grew to recognize that he was a sinner who needed to repent and find forgiveness.

Now, as a follower of Jesus Christ who was committed to upholding Christian values, Mark had to reconcile his ethics with the expectations of his team members at work. He talked it over with Annette, who struggled with the implications of what Mark felt he had to do. Her concern wasn't really that they would lose the "benefits" of the extra goods – they could handle that. She was concerned about the relationships with Mark's colleagues – and she had good reason for her apprehension. By the time Mark spoke confidentially to his supervisor, the fact that he had become a Christian was well-known. His colleagues were even gossiping about how "the new Mark" would behave, since few of them had any interest in religion. "Alf, I'm not condemning anyone and I don't intend to judge any man – but I can't condone what goes on here anymore. I don't expect things to change to suit me, so I'll look for another job." Alf did not want to lose a first-class team member, but he also quietly resented what Mark was implying. Mark's insinuation offended what Alf regarded as the team's high "moral code". Following some heated discussion, they agreed to differ. While part of Mark would have liked to stay in this job and be a witness, he told Alf that he intended to leave after his two-month period of notice.

Mark didn't find it easy to get another job, and there was some evidence of a "whispering campaign" against him over why he had left the fire service. Some mean-spirited people misinterpreted what he had intended to be a discreet exit. Mark was starting to experience some of what the Bible describes as "the offence of the cross". Fortunately, many Christian friends supported him and quite literally lived through this difficult experience with him. Mark had never felt so assured that he was taking the right course of action. He was therefore settled in his resolve and worked hard in his new job in corporate security to make sure that his family was not disadvantaged in any way. He received God's blessings with gratitude and enjoyed a new sense of peace and contentment in his life. And Annette was the first to notice this and be moved to find out more about Jesus for herself.

Throughout this chapter we have touched on many issues associated with faith and doubt. Here is a delightfully simple, anonymous poem that links them with great clarity.

Food for thought:

"Many read the Bible the way a mouse tries to remove the cheese from a trap: without being caught." (Soren Kierkegaard) How would you characterize your search for God? Are you willing to be "caught in the act" so that you can be transformed by God? Are doubts more comfortable for you than contemplating lifestyle changes and new decisions? Take some time to reflect on these questions.

III

New Foundations

7

How do I become a Christian?

"Without somehow destroying me in the process, how could God reveal himself in a way that would leave no room for doubt? If there were no room for doubt, there would be no room for me." Frederick Buechner

"Let us then approach the throne of grace with confidence, so that we may receive mercy and find grace to help us in our time of need."
(Hebrews 4:16)

Outline

New foundations: What do people build their lives upon? What is the foundation of your life?

Glimpses of God: God reveals aspects of himself to each one of us in different ways.

Steps on the way to Jesus: The process that leads to faith in Jesus.

Paul: A destroyer of Christians experiences a remarkable transformation.

Life stories: How two people found Jesus – and the story of a third who never did.

New foundations

What is the foundation of your life? Many people find such a query elementary – yet unreasonable and unanswerable. "Who knows?" you might think, or even "Who cares?" We tend not to inspect the foundations of anything very regularly. Experts study the ground conditions, the nature and scale of the structure, building regulations and so on as they plan the foundation for a building – before they ever do any construction. Once completed, the foundations are largely forgotten, unless problems become evident and cracks appear because of poor workmanship or unstable ground conditions; or an additional building development requires them to be strengthened; or a catastrophic event, such as a flood or an earthquake, exposes them. For the sake of comparison with the spiritual foundations of your life, we will call three conditions instability, building strength and catastrophe.

Few people would claim that their lives are built on solid spiritual foundations. Indeed, relatively few would say such foundations are even necessary. If they did think about foundations they would probably think in terms of cultural values: the ability to see beauty in the arts; the appreciation of the "finer things in life"; or the capacity to be in harmony with nature. Others might see as foundational the dedicated, lifelong support for a particular sports team; a passion for leisure pursuits; or the accumulation of wealth. Very few people would measure foundations in terms of God or worship. It's all too easy to live life without spiritual foundations – until a crisis comes along. Let's look at the three foundation problems we identified from a spiritual perspective.

Instability. With no warning, the ground beneath Bill's feet shifted and his life crashed down around him. The foundation of marital trust collapsed when his wife sent a message from the Maldives saying that she was on holiday with one of his best friends. For Joe, it was health – he had assumed that he was invincible until he was diagnosed with a chronic illness. For Leo, the discovery that his business partner had been defrauding him for years led to the liquidation of all his assets within six months. All three were amazed at how quickly and how radically life changed. Bill looked for the solution in a bottle; Joe was fortunate to have a great support team of friends as he battled his illness; and Leo castigated himself for placing so much trust in his colleague and suffered from depression for years. In short, they all looked for a way to repair and replace their foundations, but it was a long struggle. None of these three men had ever prayed much before, but in crises they found themselves offering up regular, faithless prayers. Bill asked a Christian friend he knew, "Please pray for me. I pray every night, but I don't believe and don't expect a response. I wish I had your faith".

Building strength. When pressures, both known and unknown, put stress on foundations that seem stable, disaster results. George Jordan was the supreme salesman. He could sell anything to anybody, or so it appeared for a while. He made incredible promises to his internet and mail order clients regarding supplies from his sports goods distributorships, and somehow he managed to fulfil them. The business expanded at an astonishing speed and George pulled in many of his friends as employees and customers. He changed the name of the company to Jordan Sports Limited – "where every promise is fulfilled". All of this was great on the surface and the Jordans enjoyed their affluence. But the business was poorly controlled and things started to go wrong on a grand scale. George defaulted on contracts with a local authority which had over one hundred schools, and with a major national group of sports and leisure centres to whom he was supplying their own branded products. In these two cases the goods were not delivered simply because they did not exist. The foundations of his promises fell apart – and recrimination, litigation and financial ruin followed. George lamented, "My word was everything – now it's nothing but a liability. It will be years before anyone in business takes my promises at face value again."

Catastrophe. Earthquakes can destroy entire buildings, including their foundations – smashed to pieces and strewn over a wide area. Foundations that were once horizontal lie at crazy angles and the surrounding area looks like a moonscape. The victims' lives as they knew them come to an end. Physical, mental and spiritual rebuilding are all essential and often take a painfully long period of time.

Catastrophes, however, happen in the lives of ordinary people every day. And so the question we want to ask is this: "If and when foundational problems occur in your life, can a personal relationship with Jesus Christ help you?" If I did not firmly believe that Jesus can help in any and every situation, I would never have written a word of this book. God has given me foundational support in many times of crisis. How? He has allowed me to see myself, and his plan, in context; he has loved me through these crises; he has brought hope where there could have been despair; he has given me a sense of blessing where others could not think that possible. But, you may say, "Fine, that's great for you – you're a Christian and you believe." But this is what a loving and engaged God offers to all of his people everywhere.

We don't always understand why. As Philip Yancey reminds us, however: "We remain ignorant of many details, not because God enjoys keeping us in the dark, but because we do not have the facilities to absorb so much light . . . Not until history has run its course will we understand how 'all things work together for good for them who love the Lord.' Faith means believing in advance what will only make sense in reverse."[73]

Reflection:

Take some time out to list the different relationships, assumptions, choices and possessions that form the foundations of your own life. How will your foundation stand up to instability, pressure or even catastrophe?

Glimpses of God

You don't need to talk to many followers of Jesus to be amazed by the diversity of ways they found him. Similarly, God uses different events to bring each person to a moment of decision to build him into the foundations of their lives. The mountaineer is suddenly dumbstruck by the magnificence of the vista that unfolds before him as the mist clears from the summit – and he sees God's handiwork as never before. The art lover is broken before the portrait of Jesus Christ that hangs before her as, for the first time, the pathos of the cross becomes real to her. The music lover who has sung Handel's "Hallelujah Chorus" for years suddenly realizes that the Redeemer does actually live and will again stand on earth. The father witnesses the pain and wonder of the birth of his perfectly formed child and marvels at the power of God's design. The gardener looks at a rose and realizes that such perfection is beyond all human skills and technology. For others, the "moment of truth" comes while

---

[73] Yancey, *Seeing in the Dark*, pp. 200, 201.

reading the Bible, hearing a sermon or the witness of a colleague, engaging in a conversation with Christians, singing a song and so on. The list is endless. You can expect to hear from God anytime. His methods are never predictable (as we saw in the life stories in Chapter 3, above).

There are, however, common elements in the process that finally leads a seeker to become a believer. The Bible sets these out for us, as we will see below. Moreover, while we may see God in many things, the message and the messenger are one: namely, Jesus Christ. We can be moved by what we see, hear and feel about God and still not have faith in Jesus. The following verses from the New Testament book of Hebrews set Jesus' role in context. "In the past God spoke to our ancestors through the prophets at many times and in various ways, but in these last days he has spoken to us by his Son, whom he appointed heir of all things, and through whom he made the universe."[74] God calls us to move from the power of sin to the power of Jesus, from darkness to light, from the worship of idols to the worship of the living God.

Steps on the way to Jesus

Table 7.1 sets out the five essential steps that are part of everyone's journey from seeker to believer. While we may become aware of God in many different ways, everyone who chooses to follow Jesus must take these essential steps. The Bible is very clear about this. First, you have to hear and understand the "good news". Many have heard a lot about Jesus, but not the good news. The Bible uses these words to refer to the whole story of the origins, birth, teaching, life, death, resurrection and ascension of Jesus Christ. The good

---

[74] Hebrews 1:1–2.

news is an integrated whole, not to be added to or subtracted from. Second, you need to formulate your own response to the good news. You may respond immediately when you hear it for the first time with conviction, or you may reject it, or you may defer your response. While we communicate with people in many different ways – we may pride ourselves on being direct or subtle, and we communicate with body language and other non-verbal methods as well as words – responding to God is quite different. We need no words since he knows our hearts. You may think you are still formulating a response to the good news, while God has already registered your response. But, if you've rejected God, it's not too late to change your response.

Table 7.1 Steps on the way to Jesus

Step	Characteristics
1 Hear the good news	We may hear the message from many different sources and by various methods. We can hear the good news many times without truly hearing or understanding it.
2 Formulate a response	This can be positive or negative. There are three basic types of response – conviction; rejection; deferral. We need to direct our response to God, not people. It's tempting to "shoot the messenger".
3 Conviction – repentance and confession	The Spirit of God brings an awareness of sin and creates a desire for confession and repentance – perhaps as

	never experienced before. This is the critical step to faith in Jesus. It may come after years of rejection and deferral, and some wrestle with conviction over long periods.
4 Acceptance and empowerment	Here the seeker gladly accepts God's remedy for sin through Jesus' death and resurrection. The new believer is freely forgiven all things! The Spirit of God enters the person and he or she becomes "a new creation in Jesus Christ".
5 Making Jesus Lord of your life	This requires a conscious act of the will. The Christian has to acknowledge Jesus Christ as not just having made a vital contribution to his or her life, but as his or her new Lord and Master – whose will comes first.

The third step is critical since it involves confession of guilt and repentance – both things we all find it difficult to do. We need to recognize how we have deliberately broken our relationship with God through our sin before we can understand and accept the forgiveness that Jesus offers. We see this central principle in the first recorded words of Jesus as he begins his ministry. "'The time has come,' he [Jesus] said. 'The kingdom of God is near. Repent and believe the good news!'"[75] Here Jesus begins his manifesto. Repentance and faith are at the heart of it.

[75] Mark 1:15.

The fourth step involves excitement and celebration for two parties. The sinner joyfully accepts Jesus as his or her Saviour. The Father, Son and Holy Spirit also collectively rejoice as a new person comes into the kingdom of God. Many people find the second of these celebrations impossible to comprehend and improbable – that God would rejoice over *you*! – but that is exactly what the Bible teaches.

The final step in this process is crucial, although many forget it. In the earliest days after Jesus' death and resurrection, the Christian church grew and flourished before the New Testament documents were available to everyone. So the church shared word-of-mouth accounts of Jesus' ministry and creedal statements, one of the earliest of which was "Jesus Christ is Lord". These words summarized the essence of the new message – the place that disciples knew Jesus wanted them to give him in their lives. "Jesus Christ is Lord" implies many things – a relationship of obedience (servant to master); a desire to follow instructions (teacher to disciple); a commitment to worship (as a worshipper to a god); a submission to a command (as a subject to his ruler). All of these rich pictures suggest what Jesus expects from us. This declaration is built into one of the most important confessional verses in the New Testament. "'The word is near you; it is in your mouth and in your heart,' that is, the word of faith we are proclaiming: That if you confess with your mouth, 'Jesus is Lord,' and believe in your heart that God raised him from the dead, you will be saved."[76] Let's look now at how some people have gone through the process of these five steps to Jesus.

---

[76] Romans 10:8–9.

Reflection:

Where would you place yourself in Table 7.1, above? Do you find yourself stuck at one of these steps and unable to move forward? If so, why do you think this is?

Paul

1. Paul: From hostility to powerful ministry

In the very early days of the church, Saul (later Paul) emerged as its most aggressive persecutor. He was an improbable convert to Christianity. He first appeared in the New Testament endorsing the stoning of Stephen, the first Christian martyr. Saul led a pogrom against the church, searching the city house by house and imprisoning Christians when he found them. He had heard the "good news", which he thought was a dangerous heresy he needed to help destroy. It is not hard to imagine, given Saul's strict religious background as a Pharisee, and his elite education, the kind of stumbling blocks that confronted his path to faith in Jesus. Jesus claimed to forgive sins – the unique function of God. Jesus offended many of the Jewish rulers by not adhering to their versions and interpretations of the Law – further, Jesus criticized many of their practices as reflecting their blindness and hypocrisy. Saul probably took the lead in many heated discussions concerning what to do about this dangerous new religious force that had emerged in Jerusalem after the reported resurrection of Jesus Christ. Saul was a man of action and willing to take whatever steps were necessary. He had formulated his response to Jesus – namely to destroy anyone who associated with him. And he did so in the name of God.

Given Saul's background and attitudes, it was going to take something extraordinary to arrest his attention and lead him to understand who Jesus really was. On his way to Damascus, apparently to gain permissions to extend his destructive campaign, a light from heaven and the voice of Jesus broke through his spiritual blindness. "'Who are you, Lord?' Saul asked. 'I am Jesus, whom you are persecuting,' he replied."[77] He was blinded (physically) and fasted for three days. No one else who was present saw anything, but they heard the voice and remained speechless. God then immediately encourages Christians, the very people Saul had been persecuting, to regard him as a co-worker. "This man is my chosen instrument to carry my name before the Gentiles and their kings and before the people of Israel. I will show him how much he must suffer for my name." [78] Fear and scepticism continued to surround Saul as he began his new career.

I have often wondered how his Jewish peers regarded Saul's dramatic transformation. Many of them would have been angered because his defection was so high profile and some would have felt betrayed. Their hostility dogged his ministry, and they threatened his life on more than one occasion. Saul's life shows us that having a radical change of heart as a result of God's intervention can have dramatic implications. Although God's plan does sometimes involve us in radical and dramatic events, the processes of conviction, repentance and conversion are always the same. After God spoke audibly to Saul, surely the almost supernatural qualities of the Christians – as they forgave and embraced the one who had so violently persecuted them – continued to reveal God's true nature to him. Probably he wondered, too, about this sacrificial willingness to die. He may have even seen Jesus and heard his preaching. Saul wholeheartedly accepts the Messiah, becomes one of his most loyal followers

---

[77] Acts 9:5.
[78] Acts 9:15–16.

and plays a pivotal role in establishing the church – both through his powerful preaching and writing some of its earliest literature.

Culturally, most of us come from very different backgrounds than Saul. But in our own way many of us harbour hostility towards Jesus. Religious prejudice and tradition shaped his perspective such that Saul was blinded to the reality of Jesus. Saul was looking for a Messiah, but not one who died in shame on a cross.

Reflection:

Do you harbour any hostility towards the church? God? Jesus? If so, try to trace its roots. Is there some hurt you can forgive, in light of what we have been saying about God's love and what Jesus has done for us? What are the consequence of continuing to allow this hostility to blind you and harden your heart?

Life stories

2. The Pearson's long march

Joe Pearson, forty-five, had a flourishing architectural practice in an affluent country town. There was no shortage of high-quality, profitable commissions and he and his team had developed an excellent reputation in restoration work. Churches, stately homes and fine mansions all over the country called for the services of Pearson and Associates. The firm had won several competitions and received many citations, accolades and awards, of which Joe was justifiably proud. His wife Irene was a general medical practitioner in a neighbouring town, and both were part of the community in which they lived. They had no children of their own but worked passionately for children's charities both at home and abroad, including an AIDS clinic in a township near Cape Town, South Africa, which they visited every year. Many admired their dedication to philanthropy, which was based not on faith but on their heart for "charity".

Joe's work brought him into regular contact with church officials from the Christian tradition. Having no faith himself, he formed different opinions about the strength of their convictions. Some of these officials were in the business of managing monuments raised to past glories. At the other end of the spectrum were the "evangelicals", for whom the buildings were much less important, but who seemed to Joe to be single-mindedly intent on "converting" him. The former, good clients though they were, left him slightly perplexed. He was never clear whether they were maintaining a system or following a person. Although he felt a bit uncomfortable at times because he didn't want to be "converted", he found that he warmed to the evangelical Christians because they were so positive and open about their faith in Jesus. They weren't perfect people. Some let him down with stage payments for contracts and others were aggressive businessmen who demanded higher standards from his company. But they were friendly and hospitable and invited Joe and Irene to many church-related events. They attended some of these functions, especially those that were social, but they also attended church with these friends on special occasions. Joe and Irene were particularly interested in hearing reports from mission charities. One local church was noted for supporting children in Africa and South America. Over a period of nearly twenty years, Joe and Irene were affiliated in some way with three different churches in the area. Several people who attended these churches did not realize that they were neither Christian believers nor members. Joe and Irene learned the language and sang the songs. They were always courteous, but rather defensive, when church leaders and friends edged towards the question of their own faith. The common ground they had with these people, as they saw it, was the compassion and care for the needy which was part of the Christian ethic. This they could understand and support. Their home contained a lot of Christian literature that had been passed on to them and they enjoyed reading biographies of philanthropists and pioneer missionaries. In a general sense, they admired what they had heard about Jesus and his compassion towards those whom society had rejected.

So the long process of Joe and Irene's exposure to the "good news" continued. They seemed to have absorbed much of it, but only because they wanted to emulate Jesus' goodness. They agreed he was a great role model. This was their adapted version of Christianity – although they never described themselves as "Christian". One Easter morning, however, they attended a service at Saint Luke's, their favourite local church. They always felt the joy and hope that pervaded this service. The vicar spoke about every person's need to meet the personal Saviour of the resurrection. He stressed that people in Jesus' time never regarded him as merely a moral teacher – and neither do we have that option today. The three common responses to Jesus were hatred, fear or adoration. It simply wasn't valid to read the biblical accounts relating what he did and who he said he was and respond with mild approval of what he stood for. Joe and Irene both realized that they had not come to terms with who Jesus really was. Their good lives, they suddenly saw, were not enough. This "model man" had come for a much bigger purpose than they had realized – Jesus had defeated death, not survived it. And he had done this for them.

Joe and Irene experienced a new birth that Easter. They asked the vicar to meet with them after the service and he was delighted to find them both ready to confess faith in Jesus and commit their lives to him. There was no more evading the truth or polite changes of the subject. God had given them an understanding of the truth and opened their eyes, which led to confession and repentance – and a surge of joy. Their lengthy journey had come to an end, to the great delight of their Christian friends. Joe wondered how many others, like him, take bits from Jesus' teachings and leave what they don't like, or think they can ignore.

3. Emily and the Alpha course

Emily Henderson tells of her own journey to meet Jesus.

"I never thought much about religion at all. I was twenty-two, and the only thing I was looking for was more clothes and shoes from the department store where I worked – and eligible young men, of course! We were all the same in my group of friends. We went clubbing every weekend; we were casual in our relationships; we were carefree; and Monday morning usually meant a bad hangover. Was I happy? Yes, because my friends and I looked after each other. And I had enough money to spend on what I thought was important.

"At home, the only time my parents mentioned religion was to berate the fanatics on television. They hadn't set foot in a church since their own wedding, and I only went to church to go to weddings. I didn't do funerals – too scary for me! I'd never seen a Bible except in a bookshop, and even at my school there was no religious worship. I do remember a few talks on great world philosophies that bored me and left me cold. A couple of people at my school went to church, but most other students thought they were weird. I had this kind of secret admiration for the way they stuck to their guns in discussion and lived by their principles.

"I'd probably still be pretty much where I was if I hadn't heard about the Alpha course. I'd seen several adverts on buses and trains that asked the question, "What's the meaning of life?" I noticed one of these three days after Jackie, one of my closest friends, was diagnosed with breast cancer at age twenty-four. I was in total shock over this, and I began to wonder if life had a meaning at all. I can see now that it was no coincidence that, the week after that, a new colleague joined my department in the store. Jocelyn Lambert immediately struck me as being different from those around me. She was a single mum and spent a lot of time caring for her ailing parents as well. But she had a contentment that was hard to fathom and a kind of inner peace that I had never seen in anyone else. I didn't really know what peace felt like. I just lived for the next party – until Jackie's illness made me start to think.

"Jocelyn and I began to take our coffee breaks together at Starbucks. As we got to know each other better, she shared with me how she had become a Christian about six months previously – after attending an Alpha course. Jocelyn said, 'You wouldn't believe the transformation in my life since then. My husband left me over three years ago because I'd been unfaithful, and my life fell apart. I realized how foolish I'd been, but I couldn't change what happened. I reached a crisis point and couldn't imagine living anymore. If it weren't for my son, Joel, I'm sure I would have ended it all then. But everything changed when I met Jesus Christ.' I listened, spellbound, and started to wonder if it would be possible for me to find that kind of meaning for my life.

"A few weeks later, Jocelyn invited me to attend an Alpha course at a church three blocks from the store. Since it was on a week night, I could go without my girlfriends knowing. The first session really surprised me. There were lots of people around my own age and the atmosphere was very welcoming and informal. Also, the video was entertaining as well as challenging, and the course material talked about real issues and was easy to understand. I was so relieved that I could blend in with the crowd and I didn't have to say anything at all if I didn't want to. As the weeks of the course went on, I found that most of the course participants were just like me. They didn't have a strong church background but were wondering what Christianity was all about and who this person Jesus was. Most of us knew almost nothing about Jesus or the purpose of his life; had never thought about sin or judgement; or heard about the work of the Holy Spirit. None of us felt ignorant asking our leaders questions, and we had some really good discussions. My conversations with Jocelyn became more intense as I plied her with more questions that came out of the course sessions. I knew that there was something I was missing, and I was determined to find it.

"I finally began to see the truth of the message of the cross and, shortly after the last session of the course, I prayed together with Jocelyn and committed my life to Jesus. I had a new sense of joy, peace and contentment – but also some concerns. During the Alpha course I continued to meet with my old friends, but with decreasing enthusiasm. To put it simply, nothing tasted the same anymore. I couldn't hide this from the girls, so I told them about the course and the things I was learning and thinking about. They were not impressed, and in fact were quite rude and intolerant. They accused me of breaking up our friendships, of being disloyal, of judging them and of 'getting all religious' – even though they had no idea what the course was really about. I was really upset by all of this, and Jocelyn's support was so important at this stage. My friends were abandoning me, but I hadn't made many new friends yet. This changed quickly when I joined the church that Jocelyn attended and formed many deep, lasting relationships. I still see some of the girls occasionally, and I'm planning to invite some of them to the next Alpha course in our church."

Emily later married Douglas, a police officer and a new Christian as well. And she has been overjoyed to be able to introduce three of her friends to Jesus.

4. God and Alex Jamieson in dialogue

Following is a conversation between God and Alex Jamieson, a thoughtful but cynical man. He resists when God begins to reveal himself to him.

God: "What did you think of the glorious scenery and weather in the Swiss Alps last week?"

Alex: "It was beautiful – the spectacular outcome of complex geological processes over aeons! I don't know how anybody can quite speak of it being a spiritual experience, though. The idea that there's a Creator just doesn't make sense to me. It was the same when our baby was born last year. It was one of the best days of my life, of course, and amazing, but it's just a natural process. Some friends tried to point out that there has to be a God to create new life, but I just don't see it."

God: "I know your thoughts on this, Alex, but I designed you to relate to me. I also see your thoughts of despair, and those niggling doubts and feelings of guilt and shame. Unless you understand who I created you to be, these dark moments will only get darker."

Alex: "Actually I'm doing fine with things just as they are. Everybody has feelings like that sometimes. It's part of being human. I can deal with it."

God (2 years later): "George Amies, who's working in your laboratory now, is a Christian. I thought it would be good for you to talk to him."

Alex: "Oddly enough, I had noticed how you keep trying to tell me things about yourself in different ways. Otherwise I'd certainly never think about God, because I don't believe there is a God. George is a good guy, bright as a button and a good worker. He's very open about his Christian faith, and he's a good advert for your cause. His beliefs even affect his behaviour. He must have a lot of faith. He wants everybody to know about Jesus. He even told me the other day that everyone will recognize that Jesus is God someday. It's really heavy stuff. Sometimes I ask him hard questions, though, to see what he'll say – and he usually has answers that make sense. He says he gets his answers from the Bible. I don't see how one book could have the answer to everything, though. It just doesn't make sense. He thinks I should read it. Maybe someday I will. But probably I won't because I can't believe what I can't see. And I'm certainly not about to change who I am in the hope of something unknown happening to me."

Epilogue: The dialogue continued for many years. God continued to place people, situations and evidence in Alex's path but, even in the years before his death, Alex successfully ignored them all. "God does not force his presence upon us. When lesser gods attract, God withdraws, honoring our fatal freedom to ignore him."[79]

---

[79] Yancey, *Rumors*, p. 50.

Food for thought:

You identified above where you are on the journey in Table 7.1, as well as some of the reasons why you might be where you are. What is one thing you could do to help you move to the next stage? If you are trying to learn more about Christianity, for example, you could begin by reading through the Gospel of Mark in the New Testament and answer the question: Who does Jesus say that he is? Is there an Alpha or *Christianity Explored* course near you that you could attend? Do you have a Christian friend or colleague you could talk with and ask some of your questions about God?

8

How do I choose?

*"Perhaps we do not realize the problem, so to
call it, of enabling free wills to co-exist with
omnipotence. It seems to involve at every
moment almost a sort of 'divine abdication'."*
C.S. Lewis

*"Now this is eternal life: that they may know
you, the only true God, and Jesus Christ, whom
you have sent."* (John 17:3)

Outline

Decisions, decisions . . . : "How do I choose?" is a difficult
question to answer when we're talking about God. This chapter
works through four aspects of this decision-making process.

Developing a relationship with Jesus: As any relationship
goes through various stages, so does our relationship with
God. Seeing these stages will help you to see your current
relationship with God with greater clarity.

Why Jesus? Christians are, first and foremost, attracted to
Jesus – not to a series of events, a creed, a set of dogmas or
a church.

Stumbling blocks – heaven and hell: What is your eternal
destiny? What are the choices?

Decisions, decisions ...

Our lives are in large part founded upon past decisions. To establish new foundations, therefore, generally involves making new and different decisions. As you consider the material in this book, and as God works in your mind and heart, you are moving towards a decision – but a decision with a difference. It's like no other you will ever make.

> "You are now at a crossroads. This is your opportunity to make the most important decision you will ever make. Forget the past. Who are you now? Who have you decided you really are now? Don't think about who you have been. Who are you now? Who have you decided to become? Make this decision consciously. Make it carefully. Make it powerfully." (Anthony Robbins, business leader and motivational speaker)

Free will is a mysterious gift from God. Napoleon once said, "Nothing is more difficult, and therefore more precious, than to be able to decide." In order to help us look logically at our decision regarding God, following is a breakdown of the four types of decisions we make every day.

1. Conscious. We make conscious decisions when we are able to pause, however briefly, to make a choice between options – whether we are studying a restaurant menu, deciding what road to take at an unfamiliar junction, or choosing a birthday card for a friend.

2. Subconscious. Although our complex neural systems are always at work, some situations are so familiar that we make split-second decisions without any apparent thought – using a knife and fork at a meal; saying good morning to a colleague; getting your car started.

3. Cumulative. Sometimes, major decisions we have already made shape our subsequent choices and so it is difficult, if not impossible, to have a completely open choice

between a range of theoretical alternatives. This is often the case in a marriage, where choices about work-sharing, leisure activities and location are conditioned by the commitment that two people have made to each other. In the same way, mistakes and wrong decisions from the past can haunt the present in matters of finance, social relationships and health.

4. Calculated. This type of decision results from long-term deliberations that involve the systematic collection of data. A career change, building a house, the decision to emigrate and purchasing a car, could all fall into this category (although some will surprise us by making snap decisions about such matters!).

Where does our decision regarding God fit into these four categories? It isn't really possible to make a subconscious decision to place faith in Jesus. Although some who grow up in a Christian environment "drift" into an association with church, everyone needs at some point to make the faith their own – or not. While past decisions may in some sense shape our choice of whether or not to place faith in Jesus (as we seek forgiveness for past guilt, for instance, or consider what our friends or family will think of our decision), it is not truly a "cumulative" decision in the sense that it is a fresh start, establishing (or rupturing) a relationship between an individual and God. For most people, and especially for adults, it is a calculated decision arrived at over time. No one can make this decision based on a complete understanding of every aspect of Jesus' teaching, knowing fully what the consequences might be, and few have followed an intense course in theology. As we have seen, this choice always involves a step of faith – into what is at least partly unknown. Jesus and the power of his love and commitment to us motivate us to respond.

Developing a relationship with Jesus

Although we cannot make a direct comparison between our relationships with other people and our relationship with Jesus, all relationships do have certain components in common. Table 8.1 breaks down the various stages of relationships to help us see more clearly where we are in relation to God. There are also important differences between human interaction and divine-human interaction. For example, God may be a stranger to you since you have no previous knowledge of him, but God knows all about you. You may have had "exchanges" with God through reading this book, as you have discovered things about him that you did not know or had not thought about. God's perspective is eternal, though, and the relationship will never end on his side. He continues to reach out to reveal more of himself to us. Reaching "common ground" is the crux of this relationship, but the distinction at this stage in our relationship with God is that we come to see things his way. We don't negotiate or strike bargains with him, because he cannot compromise.

Table 8.1 The development of a relationship

Strangers	Two people meet or are introduced for the first time
Exchanges	The two parties find out about each other – through conversation or some other sources over a period of time. These exchanges may lead nowhere or to a firm and lasting friendship.
Common ground	If the friendship progresses beyond the casual and occasional, the two people explore

	common interests, discover mutual friends and find ways of interacting socially.
Building comfort	The friendship deepens as people talk, share, help and engage in mutual support. Dependence and interdependence emerge as trust is established and reinforced. Two friends at this stage exchange inner thoughts and confidences.
Intertwined lives	The two parties are inseparable. While they interact with many others, their relationship is distinctive and this is clear to all who know them. The relationship endures the test of time, survives "ups and downs" and strengthens both individuals.

While the notion of "building comfort" is not an adequate description of a relationship with God, deepening trust, dependence and interdependence do flow directly from faith. Two-way conversations through prayer and Bible study are part of this, as is sharing experiences with other Christians. The goal of the Christian life is this intertwining of one's life with God.

But how do you achieve this deep and lasting relationship? The first step, as we have seen, is to choose to follow him. We will look now at the factors that are likely to influence your choice.

Reflection:

Could your interaction with God so far be described as a "relationship"? Has it begun to change at all? Are you still unsure as to whether or not you need Jesus? Is placing faith in someone else a problem because you have made your own way for so much of your life?

Why Jesus?

Perspective. Let's begin with God's perspective on who Jesus is and what he came to do. This verse comes from Paul's letter to the church at Ephesus, where he is listing the spiritual blessings that come for Christians through faith in Jesus. "And he [God] made known to us the mystery of his will according to his good pleasure, which he purposed in Christ, to be put into effect when the times will have reached their fulfilment – to bring all things in heaven and on earth together under one head, even Christ."[80] In other words, God has revealed himself to us through his Son Jesus, who took on human flesh and sacrificed himself so that we can have eternal life. Throughout the Bible, God emphasizes Jesus' supremacy above all things as God's ultimate purpose for the universe unfolds.

Two thousand years later, around a third of the world's population pays allegiance to Jesus, such has been his impact. Even the historian H.G. Wells, who was not a Christian, said, "The historian's test of an individual's greatness is 'What did he leave to grow? Did he start men thinking along fresh lines with a vigour that persisted after him?' By this test Jesus stands first."

Jesus' entry. It is paradoxical that, at the time that Jesus was born, Caesar Augustus had reunited his empire after civil war. He described his benign reign as "good news" (the word for "gospel"), and many thought that this was the beginning of a new world order. It was – but not under Caesar! Something amazing was happening elsewhere. Jesus was about to reveal to the world what God was really like, and this revelation began with his birth. For example, no one regarded "humility" as a virtue, and especially for a god, but this God did. In the context of the day, Jesus' birth could

---

[80] Ephesians 1:9–10.

scarcely have been humbler. Jews were fearful in their worship of God, and their access to him was strictly regulated. Jesus transforms all of this. Access to God is available to all people at all times through Jesus. Jesus introduces reverent but more familiar language. He demonstrates the practical and personal and powerful love of God. He gives care and attention to the poor and needy and those that the rest of society devalued and shunned. He developed these links from his birth and practised them in his early years in a peasant community. Jesus' entry into this world is truly remarkable, because God laid aside his glory and came to a fallen world in human form – knowing that Jesus, God's own Son, would be rejected. C.K. Chesterton observed that "Alone of all creeds, Christianity has added courage to the virtues of the Creator." In a real sense, God took a risk in sending Jesus.

His personality. Jesus experienced joy and sorrow; laughter and tears; love and righteous anger. He was a man of passion and charisma. There is a sharp contrast between his patience and gentleness towards needy and vulnerable individuals and his strident criticism of injustice and religious bigotry. He was a man of exceptional inner strength who was not afraid to weep openly in the presence of his disciples. Nor was he slow to praise people for their faith in God. Though he was God, he modelled complete humility. There is perhaps no better example of his humility than his washing his disciples' feet at the Last Supper before his crucifixion. This cleansing and welcoming act was regarded as so degrading that even a master would not demand it from a Jewish servant. By his action, therefore, Jesus – Son of God, master, teacher – symbolically stood social and religious convention on its head. His act of selfless service and love also prepared his disciples further to witness the cross of shame that Jesus would endure in a few hours' time. C.S. Lewis reminds us that Jesus was rooted firmly in the real world of his day and the painful reality of what he came to do. "He was not at all like the psychologist's picture of the integrated, balanced, adjusted, happily married, employed, popular citizen. You can't really be very well 'adjusted' to your world if it says you 'have a devil' and ends by nailing you up naked to a stake of wood."[81]

His teaching. The record of Jesus' temptation in the desert[82] sets the tone for his communication with many different audiences. He never abused his power. He refused, for example, the devil's taunt to turn stones to bread; he would not perform "miracles on demand" to impress and woo people; nor would he jump from a high place and save his own life for similar purposes. Rather, he strides through the pages of the gospels as a master teacher, a great storyteller, a miracle worker when miracles served to make his point. He did all of this with an authority that even his detractors found it difficult to challenge.

His teaching was radical and counter-cultural in its Jewish setting. For example, his requirement that the disciples be loyal to him above all others threw the sanctity of the family unit into question.[83] And who did he think he was, claiming to be able to forgive sin? The Sermon on the Mount is representative of the range and authority of Jesus' teaching.[84] This remarkable collection of ethical statements inverts many of our expectations. He taught that those who have nothing but humility and trust will inherit the kingdom (God's eternal blessing); that we are to love our enemies and pray for those

---

[81] C.S. Lewis, *The Four Loves* (London: Geoffrey Bles, 1969), p. 67.

[82] Luke 4:1–13.

[83] Luke 14:26.

[84] Matthew 5, 6 and 7.

who persecute us; that we are to care for the needy and not look for anything, even public recognition, in return; that we are to focus on treasures in heaven and not on earth, and so on. Most of the principles that Jesus taught are alien to our natural inclinations. But when we begin to see the world through God's perspective, instead of being limited by our own vision, we can see what Philip Yancey describes. "To people who are trapped in pain, in broken homes, in economic chaos, in hatred and fear, in violence – to these Jesus offers a promise of a time far longer and more substantial than this time on earth, of health and wholeness and pleasure and peace. A time of reward."[85] But Jesus' teachings are not just about the future. Christians are to live and apply them every day. In Jesus' words we see the sharpest of contrasts between the measures of success in this world and in the kingdom of heaven.

In contrast, J.B. Philips' "tongue in cheek" version of the Beatitudes reveals how we (and our world) think about success.

> Happy are the "pushers": for they get on in this world
> Happy are the hard-boiled: for they never let life hurt them
> Happy are they who complain: for they get their own way in the end
> Happy are the blasé: for they never worry over their sins
> Happy are the slave-drivers: for they get results
> Happy are the knowledgeable men of the world: for they know their way around
> Happy are the troublemakers: for they make people take notice of them."[86]

---

[85] Philip Yancey, *The Jesus I Never Knew* (Grand Rapids: Zondervan, 1995), p. 111.

[86] J.B. Philips, *Good News* (London: Geoffrey Bles, 1964), pp. 33–34.

Many who heard Jesus' teaching found it far too demanding and generally unwelcome. He called for personal penitence, humility and a willingness to change behaviour. Moreover, following and applying this teaching required total dependence on the Spirit's strength – and many then, as today, are unwilling to depend on anyone else. While Jesus inspired many with his idealism and vision, we can only implement his teaching after first placing our faith in Jesus and relying solely on his strength.

Jesus' miracles were an important part of his teaching, but they did not constitute the message itself. The miracles sometimes produced faith in those who witnessed them, but many were suspicious of them in his time and still are today. Philip Yancey helps set the miracles in context: "Jesus never met a disease he could not cure, a birth defect he could not reverse, a demon he could not exorcise. But he did meet sceptics he could not convince and sinners he could not convert. Forgiveness of sins requires an act of will on the receiver's part, and some who heard Jesus' strongest words about grace and forgiveness turned away unrepentant."[87] Since Jesus' mission was (and is) to bend our wills to his, he will only achieve a certain degree of this by external displays of power. Jesus' truth needs to sink deeply into our hearts and minds.

His death: Before and after. While we looked at the cross and resurrection in detail in Chapter 2, here we will look at some of the things that happened before and after in order to better understand how momentous these events were. The pre-cross headlines read "Hosannah: Son of God Enters Jerusalem in Triumph". Less than a week later, the headlines bring us very different news of the same man "Crucify! Crowds Shout as Son of God Dies on Golgotha". The masses

---

[87] Yancey, *Jesus I Never Knew*, p. 172.

were fickle and words were cheap then – as they are now. But Jesus was betrayed not only by the anonymous masses. Both Peter and Judas, two of his closest disciples, also betrayed him. Both of these men had listened to Jesus' teaching throughout his public ministry. They had witnessed the miracles. They called him Master. How did these betrayals make Jesus feel? Jesus demonstrates amazing grace when Peter repents. Judas, who betrayed Jesus to the authorities at his capture, brings great sorrow to Jesus. Could Jesus have forgiven him? Jesus can, and will, forgive anything and everything of which we truly repent. But, although Judas gets upset by the consequences of his sin (he returns the money he was paid and commits suicide), his heart remains hard and he does not do the one thing that could have saved him – he does not turn to his Master in repentance, and so Jesus is unable to restore relationship with him. Peter became a pillar of the early church, which demonstrates Jesus' insight into the potential of his followers as well as his willingness to forgive. God's grace is always amazing!

Just before his betrayal, Jesus spent hours of anguish in the garden of Gethsemane. We can glimpse here the true pain of bearing sin, of separation and of loneliness that Jesus was about to face. There is never anything contrived or half-hearted about Jesus, including his realization that he is about to drink a cup of profound and unimaginable suffering. Meanwhile, both his disciples and the world had rejected him.[88] If we are ever in doubt about the reality of the cost of our own sin, we see it here in Jesus' anguish before and at the cross. John Stott has observed that "We will never see the cross as something done for us, until we see it as something done by us."

---

[88] Mark 14:32–42.

After Jesus' death and resurrection, he ascended into heaven. It is crucial to understand the significance of his ascension. Jesus made it clear to his disciples (although many failed to understand) that he came to complete his work and then he would return to his Father, at which point he would pass on his mission to others. He would not leave them on their own to carry out this work but would give them the Holy Spirit to empower them. "But I tell you the truth: It is for your good that I am going away. Unless I go away, the Counsellor (Holy Spirit) will not come to you; but if I go, I will send him to you."[89] All who believe in Jesus receive the empowerment of the Holy Spirit to take part in God's mission here on earth. The Spirit brings you to Jesus and then makes it possible for you to live as a Christian in a hostile world. We see this amazing promise in action at the end of Mark's Gospel: "After the Lord Jesus had spoken to them, he was taken up into heaven and he sat at the right hand of God. Then the disciples went out and preached everywhere, and the Lord worked with them and confirmed his word by the signs that accompanied it."[90]

His work today. Christians, Jesus' disciples today, continue his work of building his kingdom. Jesus helps us to understand this invisible, spiritual kingdom in parables. It is like sowing seeds, the quiet growth of the small mustard seed into the largest tree and the search for, and purchase of, a fine pearl.[91] This kingdom has no national boundaries, no racial or cultural distinctions or demarcations based on wealth or education. The one characteristic that knits Jesus' followers together and is the foundation of his kingdom is love. Jesus said, "A new command I give you: Love one another. As I

---

[89] John 16:7.

[90] Mark 16:19–20.

[91] You can read these parables in Matthew 13.

have loved you, so you must love one another. By this everyone will know that you are my disciples, if you love one another".[92] Jesus never sets easy standards. The church is far from perfect, and you may have plenty of experiences to confirm that. The world is full of sinners who fail and make mistakes, and so is the church. The difference is that Christians acknowledge they need a Saviour – and God equips them to live in the light of that and practice repentance and love. This process of transformation can be slow and difficult. While we will never see complete transformation to perfection in this world, Jesus taught his disciples to pray that "God's will be done on earth as it is in heaven" – and he told them to concentrate first on their own lives and hearts. It is telling that, as the Christian church continues the work of Jesus, "Across the globe, faith is flourishing mainly in places where the physical world is not working out so well, where poverty and hardship press people to look for hope and meaning somewhere else."[93] Will we, though, find eternal hope and meaning in our jobs, possessions and comfortable lifestyles?

Reflection:

What have you learned about Jesus? How will this affect your choice about whether or not to follow and trust him?

Stumbling blocks – Heaven and hell

Virtually every major world religion teaches some form of reward or punishment based on how individuals live their lives. Most people with no faith in any god still have an innate sense

---

[92] John 13:34–35.

[93] Yancey, *Rumors*, p. 167.

of ultimate justice and trust that, after death, wrongs will be put right and good will eventually triumph over evil. Yet the idea that heaven and hell both exist causes many people problems. The thought that a loving God would let anyone suffer eternal punishment offends a lot of us. But both heaven and hell are important components of Christian doctrine. While the Bible is in general restrained when speaking about life after death, it tells us enough to require us to take action. We know that each of us has a soul that is eternal and will live forever in one of these two places. The poet Henry Longfellow knew that "From dust thou art to dust returneth was not spoken of the soul." The body decays, the soul does not.

Stumbling block number 7: Heaven

The central biblical truth about heaven is that Christian believers will spend eternity with Jesus Christ. The Bible describes heaven variously as "a high and holy place";[94] "a better country";[95] "the Holy City . . . [that] shone with the glory of God".[96] Those who go there they will be "richly rewarded";[97] receive a "crown of righteousness";[98] and experience endless joy, for God "will wipe every tear from their eyes. There will be no more death or mourning or crying or pain".[99] Heaven has nothing to do with angels playing harps on fluffy clouds and everything to do with being in God's presence, full of joy and life and love for ever.

[94] Isaiah 57:15.
[95] Hebrews 11:16.
[96] Revelation 21:10–11.
[97] Hebrews 10:35.
[98] 2 Timothy 4:8.
[99] Revelation 21:4.

The Bible gives us enticing glimpses of the wonders of heaven, and it also states very clearly who will go there. Jesus tells us that only those who are convinced of their own spiritual poverty and know the only solution to their problem is to turn to Jesus for forgiveness will go to heaven. (See also Table 7.1 in Chapter 7, above.) True humility is essential to seeing the need for God's remedy for sin and repenting.

Jesus spoke plainly to Nicodemus, a senior religious leader: "I tell you the truth, no-one can see the kingdom of God without being born again."[100] It is not about adopting a series of moral standards but about a fresh start, a "new birth". It involves a spiritual miracle, a total reorientation of a life, which only God can perform. This is the miracle of God's grace – without it no one can be in heaven. Jesus had much to say about the superficial religious fervour of many of the religious leaders of his day. He regarded it as a self-satisfying, hypocritical sham and no substitute for true faith.

The Bible also identifies those who will go to hell – those who have not come to Jesus for forgiveness of sin. Many of Paul's letters in the New Testament speak frankly about the permissive society of the first century and shatter any illusions that we can live exactly as we please because God will "look after us" in the end. It amazes me just how many variations on this theme can be heard today, and some of them masquerade as "Christian". The final book of the Bible, Revelation, tells us clearly that "Nothing impure will ever enter it (heaven), nor will anyone who does what is shameful and deceitful, but only those whose names are written in the Lamb's book of life."[101] The book of life referred to here contains the names of those who have repented – so that the

---

[100] John 3:3.
[101] Revelation 21:27.

sacrificial blood of Jesus "covers" their sins. These are uncompromising words, but clarity is necessary on this critical subject. This is God's prerequisite to your being in heaven.[102]

Stumbling block number 8: Hell

Some people think that judgement and hell are not central to the Christian faith. Most New Testament teaching on hell, however, comes from Jesus. In fact, Jesus talks more about heaven and hell than he does about almost any other topic. And over half of his forty or so parables are on the subject of God's eternal punishment of sinners. Clearly, hell is not a fringe topic. The Sermon on the Mount contains some of Jesus' most pointed statements about hell. Hell is not a metaphor but a terrifying reality.

As there is no more sober subject than hell, speaking about it requires honesty and sensitivity. Various biblical images give us insights into its reality. For example, Jesus described hell using the word "Gehenna", the name of a local rubbish dump – a fiery, loathsome place where unclean things, carcasses and even the dead bodies of criminals were discarded. Jesus' language is strong as he condemns religious hypocrisy. "You snakes! You brood of vipers! How will you escape being condemned to hell?"[103] It is dreadful to think of God discarding those who reject him. Jesus also uses the metaphor of a prison to describe hell – but what he means by this has nothing to do with contemporary prison regimes.

---

[102] For a recent and more comprehensive book on this topic see Randy C. Alcorn, *Heaven* (Carol Stream, IL: Tyndale House Publishers, 2005).

[103] Matthew 23:33.

In hell, both body and spirit are in captivity. Jesus said to his followers, "Do not be afraid of those who kill the body but cannot kill the soul. Rather, be afraid of the One who can destroy both soul and body in hell".[104] This "prison" is a totally barren place where the inmates are without hope and without power – and there is no prospect of rehabilitation. Jesus also talks about hell being like a pit and a place of deep darkness, with no light of any kind (whether physical, mental or moral). The Bible most frequently describes hell using images of fire. The ultimate punishment for the unrepentant sinner is unspeakable pain and suffering.

Many people could suggest a long list of candidates for hell – including murderers and other criminals, warmongers, those guilty of genocide, and so on. While judgement is completely in God's hands, the Bible does tell us a lot about the population of hell. The first thing to note is that, based on Jesus' teaching, we should not assume that hell is for a minority of dreadful people with whom you would never associate. Quite the contrary, Jesus' assumption is that Christians will always be in the minority. He says, for example, "Enter through the narrow gate. For wide is the gate and broad is the road that leads to destruction, and many enter through it. But small is the gate and narrow the road that leads to life, and only a few find it."[105] Jesus also spoke strongly about the hazards of wealth. He was not against the accumulation of wealth, but he saw that it had great powers to control people's attention, to be distracting and destructive to spiritual interests. Jesus spoke of the "deceitfulness of wealth" and, shocking though it might seem, he taught that the wealthy man ran a higher risk of being in hell than those with fewer means. But in all of this it is

---

[104] Matthew 10:28.
[105] Matthew 7:13–14.

essential to remember that Jesus forgives and accepts any who come to him in faith and humility.

Some of Jesus' most sombre words concern those who make an insincere profession of faith. He cuts through pretence, self-deception and outward shows of spirituality. "Not everyone who says to me, 'Lord, Lord,' will enter the kingdom of heaven, but only those who do the will of my Father who is in heaven . . . Then I will tell them plainly, 'I never knew you. Away from me, you evildoers!'"[106]

In his letter to the Galatian Christians Paul tells us, "Do not be deceived: God cannot be mocked. People reap what they sow. Those who sow to please their sinful nature, from that nature will reap destruction."[107] And that is why I have included the consideration of heaven and hell in a chapter about choice. Your eternal destiny, whether in heaven or hell, is a matter of your choice. It's not the outcome of a sophisticated lottery process or the product of blind chance as some believe, but the direct result of your obedience or disobedience to God's will as revealed in Jesus Christ.[108]

---

[106] Matthew 7:21,23.

[107] Galatians 6:7–8.

[108] If you would like to read a more detailed book on this subject, see John Blanchard, *Whatever Happened to Hell?* (Darlington: Evangelical Press, 1993).

Food for thought:

A.W. Tozer, a famous twentieth-century Christian writer, observed that, "The vague and tenuous hope that God is too kind to punish the ungodly has become a deadly opiate for the consciences of millions."

Michael Faraday was perhaps the greatest experimental physicist of the nineteenth century. When questioned regarding his speculations on life after death he replied, "Speculations? I know nothing about speculations. I'm resting on certainties. I know that my Redeemer lives and because he lives, I shall also live."

God gives us free will. He gives us minds and hearts that are capable of either rejecting or obeying him. What do you think about the idea that God gives us a choice about how to live our lives now? And how does your perspective change when you think about God giving us our choice for eternity as well?

9

Can I handle the consequences?

"The prison has been stormed, and the gates of the prison have been opened, but unless we leave our prison cells and go forward into the light of freedom, we are still unredeemed in actuality." Donald Bloesch

"God did not keep back his own Son, but he gave him for us. If God did this, won't he freely give us everything else?" (Romans 8:32, CEV)

Outline

Actions and reactions: Just what are the consequences of following Jesus?

Breaking the cycle: Some people are fearful of what following Jesus might mean for them. How can we break through that cycle?

Handling the consequences: Life stories: The stories of three people working through the consequences of following Jesus help us to see the problems – and God's solutions.

Actions and reactions

Every event and decision has consequences, many of which are hard to predict and difficult to quantify. We can see this all around us – in the environment, in politics and social issues and so on. Debate rages, for example, over the long-term effects of deforestation on soil erosion and crop production; over the depletion of the ozone layer through the excess production of "greenhouse" gases; and over building cities on high-risk flood plains. We are witnessing the global impact of the Asian tsunami in 2004, and the many damaging consequences of earthquakes and other natural disasters the world over. Social and political upheaval and conflict in places like Iraq, Chechnya, Afghanistan, Israel and Ireland set off a complex chain of actions and reactions. The world continues to reverberate from the consequences of the terrorist attack on the Twin Towers in New York on September 11, 2001. It is nearly impossible to trace all of the causes and effects of world poverty, corrupt governments, poor distribution of global resources, fluctuating commodity prices and so on.

Many people spend a lot of time and effort calculating the consequences of actions they have taken, or plan to take. From what we have said thus far about the transforming truth of Christianity, you might think that no one who was seriously considering placing faith in Jesus would bother to spend much time worrying about the reactions of others. But we cannot underestimate the scale of this stumbling block for some. "What tensions will this fuel in my immediate family?" "How will applying a new set of values affect my business and relationships with colleagues?" "Will God help me to achieve the kind of reconciliation that I long for among my extended family, many of whom I've treated so badly over the past two decades?" Many remain frozen in a state of inertia as they weigh up the consequences of their next move. They may hover for years at the edge of faith, keeping a certain distance from Jesus as they are attracted by him and also distracted by the potential reaction of others. What does it take to break such a cycle?

Jesus laid out his expectations of the disciples very clearly, and he also set out some of the consequences that those who chose to follow him might suffer. He pulls no punches. The first such consequence concerns families. Jesus did not come to break up families, but he did want to establish a clear sense of new priorities in his followers. "Anyone who loves father or mother more than me is not worthy of me; anyone who loves son or daughter more than me is not worthy of me. Those who do not take up their cross and follow me are not worthy of me."[109] Paul explains, by word as well as by example, the various trials that Christians endure. Paul writes, "We sent Timothy, who is our brother and God's fellow worker in spreading the gospel of Christ, to strengthen and encourage you in your faith, so that no-one would be unsettled by these trials. You know quite well that we were destined for them. In fact, when we were with you, we kept telling you that we would be persecuted. And it turned out that way, as you well know".[110] Finally, the Bible tells Christians that they will experience persecution and face insults in the name of Jesus. Notice, however, the strong note of joy in these verses. "Rejoice that you participate in the sufferings of Christ, so that you may be overjoyed when his glory is revealed. If you are insulted because of the name of Christ, you are blessed . . . if you suffer as a Christian, do not be ashamed, but praise God that you bear that name."[111]

---

[109] Matthew 10:34–38.

[110] 1 Thessalonians 3:2–4.

[111] 1 Peter 4:13–14,16.

But the Bible also gives us plenty of encouragement in the face of any consequences. "May the God of hope fill you with all joy and peace as you trust in him, so that you may overflow with hope by the power of the Holy Spirit."[112]

Reflection:

Do you have particular reasons to fear any of these potential consequences of choosing to follow Jesus? If you do, try to list them and talk to a Christian friend about them.

Breaking the cycle

How is it possible for such hesitant people, who spend so much time going over and over the pros and cons of faith, to take the final step?

You have to be convinced about the quality of the leadership. Is God truth? Can you trust him to lead you through whatever lies ahead? Unless you know the reality of the God who calls you to trust him, you will try to work out the consequences on your own. You cannot take a step of faith into the unknown without trusting who God is. You can have mentors, prayer partners and friends, but only God can be your leader.

You have to be willing to be trained for the battle. Many people hesitate about becoming Christians because they don't feel equipped to handle the consequences. Some look at Christians who seem able to cope with tremendous difficulties and then make comparisons with their own situations. While everyone receives the power of the Spirit at conversion, not only has God created us as unique individuals, he also equips us in different ways for different

---

[112] Romans 15:13.

tasks. I have known many people God has equipped in quite remarkable ways. For example, I have known people who showed no aptitude for language study who subsequently became distinguished translators of minority, and often undocumented, languages as part of Bible translation work. I have known people (some with speech impediments) who were terrified of speaking in public, but who became outstanding communicators with God's empowerment. Others I have known have made career changes that I never would have been able to predict. More commonly, of course, God enables Christians to develop as individuals so that they can be effective disciples just where they are. God is committed to equipping you to handle the consequences of your decision.

You have to be prepared to take risks. This means you have to develop a progressively better understanding of short-term risks that are offset by medium- and longer-term rewards. When Christians make important decisions, part of the process is trusting God to take care of the apparent "risks". These include being misunderstood; not being accepted by friends, family or peers; developing new relationships in an established Christian community, and a host of other matters that are specific to your own situation.

You have to be convinced of the need to fight. We can all think of people who display incredible courage and tenacity in conquering adversity: the cancer victim who runs marathons for charity; the bereaved mother who reaches out to support others in similar circumstances; refugees who survive against all the odds. Many others, however, display very little fighting spirit to make personal relationships work – if soaring divorce rates are anything to judge by. We give in to getting caught up in petty disputes of all kinds; we abdicate our responsibilities to care for others in need; we observe all sorts of injustice with detachment; we let go of our dreams because we just can't be bothered. If it is worthwhile, however, it is worth fighting for. Sadly, some Christians give up the fight. Those I know who have done this generally admit that they tried to tackle too much of the fight in their own way and in their own strength. In all of this we remember how much hostility Jesus endured. He "was hated without a cause" – and, even today, his church is subject to persecution in many parts of the world. But, as we have seen again and again, victory is assured.

Reflection:

Jim Elliot, a young man who was martyred for his faith in South America, said that, "God always gives his best to those who leave the choice with him." How would that apply to you today?

Handling the consequences in real life

1. Marcus' assessment

Sir Marcus Peterson was a high-profile junior minister and a member of the UK Cabinet, with responsibility for social security and poverty. He was a rising star in the political firmament – innovative, full of policy ideas, and he frequently wrote influential pamphlets for party conferences. He was also popular as a speaker and supporter of his party at by-elections, in part because his charisma outshone the dullness of many worthy local candidates.

Marcus was a lawyer who specialized in civil cases, many of which had become very well known because they involved large-scale class actions on alleged product failures in areas such as medical products, and drugs in particular. He was a favourite within his Chambers in London's famed Inns of

Court and was likely to become its Head in the near future. Anna, his wife of ten years, was also a lawyer – in the family division of a neighbouring Chambers specializing in domestic affairs, divorce, family settlements and so on. Together they were a formidable couple with a wide range of complementary legal skills and experience.

They earned a lot of money, especially Marcus – but neither of them had much time to spend it. A good financial adviser solved this problem for them. They didn't have much time for hobbies, either. Playing some regular contract bridge was one of their few interests, and they enjoyed reading biographies and autobiographies – but mainly while on holiday. They also collected eighteenth-century English and French pottery, but largely through agents. They had no children and not much time to think about ever having them.

Marcus had contemplated a move into politics for some time before he finally sought election for a London seat when he was forty. The crusading lawyers of the past who had promoted social reform in many different countries inspired him, and he felt that this could only be effectively achieved from inside the political machine. Marcus was Conservative by inclination and, although he came to politics through a rather elitist route, his party and his constituents in the affluent West End of London regarded this positively – so he was selected at his first attempt. Some five years later, such was his evident talent that he was appointed as a junior minister in the government. An early ambition had been realized, and he made every effort to balance two careers.

Marcus had never given much thought to anything religious. He had met a number of colleagues who were members of Christian law fellowships, especially in the US. Several of them had established charitable foundations to promote social reform, and he had a high regard for them.

Describing some of them to Anna late one evening, he said, "Something quite basic has had a major influence in their lives, and I can't put my finger on exactly what it is. I feel like I've been so self-contained and focused on pursuing my own career, I haven't left time for anything else." In retrospect, Marcus saw these stirrings in his consciousness as the beginning of his journey. He had seen a "chink in his armour". His attitudes began to soften, and he had a new openness to looking at life in a different way. Friends gave him a few books by Christian legal apologists, and these fuelled his curiosity. Ernest Brentford first met Marcus at a prayer breakfast in Parliament. He saw the potential for God that lay within Marcus Peterson and began to pray for him and shared his Christian faith with Marcus over many lunches. Marcus was a fine debater, but he was also an open-minded man who sifted through the evidence fairly. Marcus and Ernest discussed many of the stumbling blocks and stepping stones we've looked at when they met.

But the biggest issue that faced Marcus took some time to resolve. In his professional and parliamentary lives he pursued the vagaries of client interests on the one hand, and pandered to political demands on the other. "If I became a Christian, how could I bring glory to God in my day-to-day living?" He had read about the concept of Christians bringing the "sacramental" into everyday life. This meant keeping the sacred ("sacra") in mind ("mental") at all times. To do this he would have to acknowledge God's presence everywhere and not separate the secular and the sacred.[113]

Marcus thought through what he could do to handle the consequences of becoming a Christian very carefully. He had come across many instances where he was far from persuaded

---

[113] Philip Yancey, in *Rumors*, p. 44, develops these ideas well.

of the merits of his client's case. Could he make it clear to clients that his values had changed and that he would pursue cases differently? Would he turn down cases for these reasons? What kind of civil lawyer would he then be? His fellow chamber members would regard this as financial recklessness. His decisions would also call some of their behaviour into question. Although he did not know what the consequences for his income would be, he was not concerned about them. In many ways the political side of his life was more problematic, because it was more public and involved so many more factions. Up to this point he had never voted against the government, even in matters where he was uneasy; nor had he spoken out about the hypocrisy he observed; he had never anticipated that he might be in serious conflict over policy. As it was, he now saw that he would have to rethink his position on several issues. His eyes were being opened.

Ernest had never seen anyone try to work out the consequences of embracing the Christian faith so thoroughly. At times he wondered if Marcus was being too clinical and was perhaps treating it as intellectual exercise for his restless mind. But he was wrong. Marcus shared his journey seeking faith with Anna every step of the way. She was supportive, but unconvinced. About five years after he began to enquire who he was, why he was here and where he was going, Marcus became a Christian. He explained to everyone how he was implementing the consequences of his choice and, in so doing, he became a powerful apologist for his new faith. His professional life flourished, although his political life did suffer. His new level of integrity drove the former, while his unwillingness to compromise changed the latter. As he lived out his faith, however, he was certain of his new joy and hope and looked to God, not human beings, for his identity and approval. Marcus was transformed and empowered by God.

2. Jordan's takeover

Jordan Melville would never forget one particular six-month period, during which business and personal changes came together in a unique way. Jordan was chief executive of Innovations plc, a public company that made delicatessen foods and employed about three thousand people throughout Europe. Jordan writes,

"It started late one night in the middle of April, when the chairman of the Innovations board called me at home. 'Jordan, I've just taken a call from Bobby Jones at European Food Products plc. They're going to announce a bid to take us over in the morning and have already informed the stock exchange to this effect. He's likely to be as aggressive as ever. So there's trouble ahead! We need to get together first thing tomorrow to decide on our response.' I didn't sleep much that night. Bobby Jones was both ruthless and successful. He was the darling of the investment community because of the returns for shareholders he had achieved in recent years. I knew that he would have done a great deal of work, and gained much support, before launching his unsolicited bid. Although we would mount a stout defence against him, he was known for offering tempting prices to shareholders and for financing them by savage cost-cutting once he took over the business. My approach to running a company was very different, and widely recognized in the trade to be different. We were not as profitable as European, and that would go against us, but we had a great reputation for first-class supplier and customer relationships, open management, employee shareholding and a consultative culture that encouraged innovation. From the outset, I knew that if the bid succeeded I would be a casualty. That didn't worry me, but I knew that hundreds of my colleagues would also be victims of his rationalization programmes, and that none of my senior team would be there to look after our employees' interests.

"The bid came and, as expected, it was a full price. We did our duty as a board, rejected it as not being high enough, and battled hard to have our alternative plans accepted by our investors. As invariably happens, that's where things become public and personal – as they had by June that year. The business press likes nothing better than sedate executives falling out. Bobby Jones warmed to the task. 'Jordan's a good man, but where were these plans to add to shareholder value before our bid? The company has lost direction under his leadership and the shareholders' confidence is at an all-time low. Everyone agrees that it would be better run if it was in our hands.' I would reply along these lines: 'We know what Bobby has achieved, but the social costs are high and he buys innovation by taking over companies with potential – and on occasion destroying that potential by his ruthless methods. His development expenditure is minimal, and if any company in this industry will run out of steam it will be his.' The public debate became ever more acrimonious as the closing date for voting approached. I found myself less and less comfortable with all of this. By September, we had lost the vote and European had over 90 per cent backing from the shareholders. All of the predictable outcomes came to pass swiftly thereafter. The takeover had completely dominated my life for six months, night and day, and I was drained, disappointed and distressed – and unemployed!

"Had another kind of 'takeover' battle not been going on in my life over a much longer period, I doubt that I would have survived the experience without a stress-related breakdown. Four years earlier, while doing a placement at our apprenticeship school graduation, the local Gideon International branch had presented me with a Bible. This was a book with which I was completely unfamiliar. I took it with me in my briefcase as I travelled around the world. I found the guidelines on various passages for different circumstances to be very helpful – although a few of them were a bit confusing and rather pointed. Other times, the verses were very clear to me and their implications unavoidable. "But seek first his (God's) kingdom and his righteousness, and all these things will be given to you as well. Therefore do not worry about tomorrow, for tomorrow will worry about itself. Each day has enough trouble of its own."[114] This message hit me hard, because I hadn't spent any time 'seeking' God. As for worry, I did that all the time and about everything. It was part of my job as I saw it. When I first read this, I was astonished that someone else would be willing, interested or capable of carrying my worries. But God was.

"The day we lost the contested takeover battle for Innovations was the blackest day ever in my professional and personal life. At that moment I felt like a complete failure, although I had many phone calls from investors who were happy about the improved price we had achieved. Some of them had made a great deal of money, and they were not complaining. I was a hero for some, but I saw myself as a villain for others – the employees in particular. They also had a financial cushion, but few would have jobs with the company – and the company they loved had, in effect, gone. I knew I was too emotional to see all this clearly at the time. But fortunately by that stage I knew where to go for assurance. I had already experienced God's goodness in my life. "Humble yourselves, therefore, under God's mighty hand, that he may lift you up in due time. Cast all your anxiety on him because he cares for you."[115] It was easy to be humbled by the powerful and dispassionate market forces that had

---

[114] Matthew 6:33–34.

[115] 1 Peter 5:6–7.

worked against me, but God's hand was quite different and he used his power with the opposite intent. It was incredible to be able to lay my burden down with him.

"This was one takeover that I welcomed with open arms. I confessed and believed and experienced the great joy of this verse: 'For God, who said, "Let light shine out of darkness," made his light shine in our hearts to give us the light of the knowledge of the glory of God in the face of Christ.'[116] I had no fears about the consequences of my decision. The publicity surrounding the European takeover paid dividends, and I was soon running a smaller food company whose chief executive had just retired. I had made a conscious decision to be very open with all my new colleagues about my Christian faith. During my first week, when introducing myself to my top forty managers, I simply told my story and explained how this would affect my running of the business. While there were a few cynics, my message was well received. My chief engineer reported a conversation that he had overheard. 'At least he has some principles, and I admire his guts. As we work with him, we'll see how consistent he is in applying them.' While I had made myself vulnerable at one level, I had every confidence that God would help me handle the consequences. And he has."

3. Pete's gamble

The Campbell family had a fairly tempestuous history. Christians within the family practiced their faith in different ways, and there was no shortage of theological disputes. At one level they seemed to treat theology very casually, but feelings ran deep about these differences of opinion. They adhered to different traditions within different

---

[116] 2 Corinthians 4:6.

denominations, but at times it was nearly impossible to see any trace of love, grace or compassion in the way they treated each other. People who knew the family would often comment that they were among the worst advocates for following Jesus Christ. Others would compare them to the hypocritical Pharisees, who treated Jesus so cruelly, and note that the Campbells failed the key test that Jesus gave us, namely that "we love one another". The roots of this disunity lay deep in the past.

Pete Campbell was the black sheep of his generation in this large extended family. He had been a gambler since his early high school years. He didn't show an aptitude for much else, but he could work out gambling odds quicker than anyone and was willing to bet on anything. He needed money to do this, however, and his compulsion drew him from petty crime into more serious criminal activity, and he became involved with ever more unsavoury characters. While his parents had been tender and very patient, every attempt to help Pete out of his addictions had failed. Christian compassion was evident, but it all became too much. As a last resort, his family disowned him while he was still a teenager. The pressures from some members of the wider family were also persistent, vocal and hurtful. By age twenty, Pete had cleaned up his life enough to get a job with a bookmaker. This was progress. He was so successful that, ten years later, he was successfully managing a group of shops and a number of casinos for a national chain. In an industry where senior people keep a low profile, by his mid-thirties Pete began to emerge as a luminary in the industry and became very visible in the media. By this time, all of the Campbell family were hoping that Pete would change his name, leave the planet or disappear from sight. But something even more amazing actually happened.

Pete had no personal contact with any of his extended family, but he did get a great deal of feedback from them about how they felt about him. For example, he received two aggressive letters of criticism from two different cousins and regular damning e-mails as part of a strange "family newsletter" which regularly featured him in totally negative terms and which was full of innuendo. The family had written Pete off as beyond redemption – at least their version of redemption. Pete was not an insensitive man and he found this vendetta from his family hard to take. With Sandra, his wife, he began to try to understand what was going on in their hearts and heads. He could understand why they were upset by his early criminal record, and by the fact that he was in a profession which was anathema to most Christians, and he knew his public visibility did not help. But it was the association of the family name, with its allegedly Christian traditions, that seemed to be at the root of many of the attitudes he encountered.

Always a gambler, Pete decided he would take the risk of his life – he would read the Bible. He remembered almost nothing he had been taught as a child, but what he did was telling. "I know that God forgives people. I don't think I need to be forgiven necessarily, but I'm prepared to look. I really want to understand my family's behaviour. It's a risk, isn't it? I'll either get nothing or come up trumps." If some of his family had known of his motivation and the way he was approaching the exercise, they would have been appalled and might even have said that nothing good could ever come of it. Pete, in turn, might have quoted odds of 10/1 against God speaking to him; and odds of 50/1 against him listening. But both were wrong. Pete never did anything by halves, so his reading over many months was thorough and careful. Gradually, he began to see a new light shining into his life.

He did need God. He was truly convicted about his sinful life, which he now regarded as wasted to a large degree.

The news quickly reached the extended family. Pete's renewed spirit was warm, generous and Christ-like. "I forgive them all," he told Sandra. "I have a lot of work to do to re-focus my life, but God will be my judge, not the Campbell family. I won't align myself with any of their factions that now I see have nothing to do with Jesus at all." Pete had already begun to think through the consequences. As he began reading the Bible and investigating the faith he gradually became convinced that he needed a different career, so he became the manager of a group of sports clubs. He told his story on the web in the "Family Newsletter". To his delight, he received a few very welcoming responses from various parts of the country. Some of them he followed up with meetings that launched new family friendships which he would never have thought possible. Some of the other replies, sadly, revealed that these so-called "Christians" were very confused indeed about God's love, grace and calling. Pete continued to grow as a Christian and became involved in a local church. In one of the books Pete read he was struck by this quote: "The state God desires for us, shalom, results in a person fully alive, functioning optimally to the Designer's specification."[117] Pete was ready for that, regardless of the consequences – peace with God, with himself, with his community and with his family.

Reflection:

What can you learn from the experiences of Marcus, Jordan and Pete? Would you have handled their situations differently? If so, how?

---

[117] Yancey, Rumors, pp. 132–33.

Food for thought:

Augustine said, "God is always trying to give good things to us, but our hands are too full to receive them." What in your life do you need to lay down so that you can receive from God?

10

What happens now?

"And the end of all our exploring
Will be to arrive where we started
And know the place for the first time."
T.S. Elliott

"God reserved for his children the priceless gift
of eternal life; it is kept in heaven for you, pure
and undefiled, beyond the reach of change and
decay." (1 Peter 1:4, TLB)

Outline

Where were you? What approach were you taking to God in Chapter 1?

What happens now? Consider your four different options: do nothing; keep looking; keep resisting; start believing.

What did they do? Three people who met Jesus in the flesh, and three who heard Paul's defence of his faith first-hand, responded very differently.

Where were you?

In Chapter 1, Table 1.2 provided some broad categories describing how different people look for God. Into which group did you place yourself? Read through the different categories in this table again to determine whether there has been any movement in your thinking, either positive or negative, in relationship to God. You may, for example, have described yourself as "casual" but have since encountered thoughts, feelings or ideas as you've read that you found disturbing, or unsettling, or that caused you to look further. Or you might have classified yourself as "eclectic" but have found that some of your views are inconsistent with one another.

Most people living in the West in the twenty-first century lead busy lives and have little time for either reading or thinking. This is part of life's struggle – and it has its consequences, one of which is that we quickly lose touch with the larger perspective. The only reality that matters for eternity, God's plan to rescue humankind through Jesus Christ, is easy to miss while we're busy living our lives in the here and now. Louis XVI was so out of touch with the affairs of his kingdom that, on the very day of the storming of the Bastille (the event that launched the French Revolution), he made an astonishing entry in his diary. Recording the events of July 14, 1789, he wrote: "Rien" (French for "nothing"). How remarkable, you might think – he was about to lose everything. Our answer regarding Jesus, however, as we have seen, cannot be "rien".

C.S. Lewis stated the question before us in very clear terms: "A man who was merely a man and said the sort of things Jesus said would not be a great moral teacher. He would either be a lunatic – on a level of a man who says he is a poached egg – or else he would be the Devil of Hell . . . You can shut him up for a fool, you can spit on him and kill him as a demon; or you can fall at his feet and call him Lord. But let us not come with any patronizing nonsense about his being a great human teacher. He has not left that open to us. He did not intend to."[118] C.S. Lewis, perhaps best known to many today as the author of *The Chronicles of Narnia*, was a man of great intellect who came to faith in Jesus Christ after a long period of seeking and weighing the biblical evidence.

What happens now?

Each person who begins to examine the evidence for Christianity, as we have done throughout this book, is faced with a choice. Following is a consideration of the four different options.

1. Do nothing

"I'm not doing anything. I only read this book because I didn't want to offend my friend who gave it to me. I understand better what Christians believe and why, but it's not for me."

"God may speak to other people, but I haven't heard from him, so there's really nothing to say or do."

"I know more about Christianity now, but I'm still struggling to see why I need this kind of radical transformation in my life. Maybe someday."

You may have similar sentiments to those expressed above. That's fair enough, but we need to look beneath the surface of comments like these so we're absolutely clear about the implications. Because we've looked at God through his own words, the Bible, "doing nothing" means that you are saying "no" to God – however kindly or graciously. You are not acknowledging who God is or what Jesus has done.

---

[118] Lewis, *Mere Christianity*, p. 56.

202 I'm Dying to Tell You

We need to understand the logical conclusion of this kind of thinking. A.N. Wilson's comment on the emergence of communism perfectly illustrates the principle. He observed, "Dethroning God, that generation found it impossible to leave the sanctuary empty. They put man in His place, which had the paradoxical effect, not of elevating human nature but of demeaning it to depths of cruelty, depravity and stupidity unparalleled in human history".[119] God designed human beings to worship. If we do not acknowledge God and worship him, we will worship something or someone else. "Doing nothing" about God, then, means that the object of worship is elsewhere. It will be helpful for you, in working out the consequences of your decision, to determine what or who it is that you worship – whether it is self, success, family, money, an addiction or habit, a relationship or something else.

2. Keep looking

"I want to find out more about sin and forgiveness because I can't understand how one man could carry all that guilt on a cross. I've started to look at my own life and wonder if Jesus really was able to take the punishment for all the things I've thought, said and done that the Bible defines as sin."

"I want to talk with someone else just like me who has the Holy Spirit living in them, because I just can't imagine what that's like."

"I'm a successful, independent person, and I think saying 'Jesus is Lord' sounds so alien. Is this an outdated concept?"

These are among the many valid questions you may be asking at this point. But it is crucial, as you continue looking,

---

[119] A.N. Wilson, *God's Funeral* (New York: W.W. Norton, 1999), p. 304.

to keep in mind who you are looking for. If, for example, you are looking for a "perfect Christian" before you trust Jesus, you will be disappointed. But if you seek to understand how Jesus transforms people's lives, seeing Christians (fellow sinners) growing in faith and love as they try to live lives that are pleasing to God, you will learn much. Similarly, if you keep looking at the life and work of Jesus Christ, you will understand more and more about who God is and who you are. It is also important to remember that it's impossible to look further without reading the Bible itself. It comes with this power-packed promise: "The word of God is living and active. Sharper than any double-edged sword, it penetrates even to dividing soul and spirit, joints and marrow; it judges the thoughts and attitudes of the heart."[120] It is possible to look without any real focus, or indeed to worry away at some theological nicety as a dog gnaws at a bone – and miss seeing the only person that matters, Jesus Christ.

The contemporary Christian writer Philip Yancey helps us again here. "We see God best in the same way in which we see a solar eclipse, not by staring at the sun which would cause blindness, but through something on which the sun is projected."[121] We see God primarily in his Son, Jesus Christ, but also in his work in nature and (provided we have properly focused expectations) in these "new creatures" who believe in him and call themselves Christians.

3. Keep resisting

"I found myself identifying with some of the people in the life stories, and I'm a bit surprised to find myself experiencing

---

[120] Hebrews 4:12.
[121] Yancey, Rumors, p. 25.

some guilt feelings about some of the choices I've made in my life. But it's not like I'm ready to surrender my life to God or anything."

"I don't know why, but since I've started reading about Christianity I keep meeting all these Christians in the most unlikely places. I feel like it's a conspiracy, and I'm certainly not giving in to it."

"I think my resistance to God has softened a bit since my wife and teenage daughter became Christians. They're both being transformed by God in some beautiful and amazing ways. I know they pray for me, but I'm not quite there yet. I think I probably still have some pride to overcome – especially since I mocked their faith quite a bit in the beginning."

Building up our resistance in some circumstances is a good thing. For example, healthy food and regular exercise help build resistance to disease. Good education and training can enable a person to resist unreasonable ideas or deception by those who try to exploit them. I once worked with some tough men in the steel industry whose jobs required them to withstand high-temperature environments in "melting shops". Their hands had developed resistance to most levels of heat so that they were rarely burned. While these types of resistance are good, however, building defence mechanisms against God is not good. It's amazing that, given God's power, such a thing is possible – but it is. God gives us free will to choose. And you may notice some evidence of resistance in your attitude to what we have considered throughout this book.

Coming to trust Jesus in faith, however, means breaking down those barriers of resistance and surrendering to him. Thomas Merton explains the benefits of this amazing process of surrender: "The gift of ourselves in total submission to God is a sacrifice in which, far from losing anything, we gain everything and recover, in a more perfect mode of possession, even what we seem to have lost. For at that very moment when we give ourselves to God, God gives himself to us."[122] Human beings are not good at surrendering to anything or anyone – in a family or social argument, in a challenging business or professional situation, or in virtually any circumstance we encounter. But every single person has an eternal problem that cannot be solved in any other way. We can resist it, but we cannot solve it ourselves; we can accept it, but we cannot negotiate it; we can postpone it, but we cannot forget it. Nothing but absolute surrender will do.

4. Start believing

"I surrender – gladly! I know that God has been revealing himself to me for years in so many ways, and I finally understand what it means to become a Christian. I'm so at peace and full of joy – and grateful for God's patience with me."

"I've run out of excuses and arguments. I still have lots of questions, but I'm beginning to understand what faith entails. So here I am!"

"I thought that I had everything worked out in my mind – how the world works and what happens when we die. But now that I've heard some of God's own words and understand his amazing rescue plan, I want to be part of it. I used to be a spectator – now I'm a believer."

God demonstrates incredible patience and gentleness over years of our inattention, indifference and hostility – and rejoices when we come to him in faith.

The heartfelt joy of new Christians never ceases to amaze and encourage me. New Christians are so full of that sense of

---

[122] Thomas Merton, *Ascent to Truth* (San Diego: Harcourt, Brace & Jovanovitch, 1951), p. 117.

discovery, wonder and gratitude that flows from experiencing God's love and forgiveness. They usually want to talk about what they are learning from the Bible, how they are sharing their faith with others, who they are praying for and where they need God's guidance in the detail of their lives.

Reflection:

C.S. Lewis reminds us that "You never know how much you really believe anything until its truth, or falsehood, becomes a matter of life and death to you." As we have seen again and again, this decision is a matter of life and death. Which of these four choices have you made?

Two worlds

Christians, who have become "citizens of heaven", will begin to see the truth of the two worlds of the Bible – the "already but not yet" of this world and the next. As C.S. Lewis grew in his faith he observed, "If I find in myself a desire which no experience in this world can satisfy, the most probable explanation is that I was made for another world."[123] The Bible consistently connects the visible and invisible worlds, and Christians need to understand the implications of these connections. History is a series of events occurring in parallel, each with a visible and invisible dimension. The main focus of attention is on the visible world, the world of sight and sound that surrounds us, and God works largely through people like ourselves. While in this life Christians will experience pain as well as blessing, joy as well as sorrow, God equips us with the strength and grace and love to face any and every trial.

---

[123] Lewis, *Mere Christianity*, p. 118.

Christians are new people "under construction" – works in progress, if you like. We have begun a new relationship here that will culminate in the invisible world. While our relationship with God is good here, it will become so much better in heaven, because the imperfections will have gone. The following verse from Paul's first letter to the Christians at Corinth explains this concept well: "Now we see but a poor reflection as in a mirror, then we shall see face to face. Now I know in part; then I shall know fully, even as I am fully known."[124] Meanwhile, as Christians we live with a consciousness of both worlds in our prayers, worship and behaviour – indeed the words of the disciples' prayer reflect that as we ask that "God's will might be done on earth as it is in heaven". So if you have now started believing, you find yourself with dual citizenship. This citizenship entails countless privileges, but it also requires Christians, with God's help, to weigh up our loyalties between earth and heaven and to resolve conflicting demands.

What did they do?

Following are some of the reactions of people who met Jesus in the flesh and/or heard the good news about him from Jesus' close followers. It is important to remember that many in the crowds who heard Jesus preach and witnessed his miracles did not respond in any positive way. That is still true today.

Reactions to meeting Jesus

While it's impossible to imagine what meeting Jesus in the flesh must have been like, through the power of the Holy Spirit we are invited to "meet" him as well. So, while the

---

[124] 1 Corinthians 13:12.

comparison has its limitations, we can learn much from the attitudes of three people who did meet him "in person".

1. Peter. "Go away from me, Lord; I am a sinful man!"[125] Peter's fishing skills had failed him that day. This was his livelihood, and he had worked all night and caught nothing. Jesus asked to use the boat of a fisherman named Simon as a floating pulpit to teach the people. Peter listened in. Jesus then instructed Peter where to go to fish – and a miraculous catch resulted. Peter's confession above was probably a response to both the power of Jesus' teaching and the power behind the miraculous catch of fish. Peter made this confession on his knees – an act of personal humbling before someone much greater than ourselves. Jesus responded to Peter with compassion and reassurance.

All of us need to approach God with penitence. He is neither a buddy nor a peer. But, when we repent, he makes us his sons and daughters, joint heirs with Jesus Christ and so much more. But the relationship has to begin "on our knees", either literally or metaphorically.

2. Levi. "'Follow me,' Jesus said to him, and Levi got up, left everything and followed him."[126] Did Levi hear Jesus' preaching before he received this life-changing call? We don't know. We do, however, know about the Roman system of tax collection. Having determined the gross sum that was to be recovered from that part of their empire, Roman authorities delegated the extraction of the payments to locals like Levi. He and others like him had ample opportunity to add to their own fortunes through this system, and the people detested tax collectors for their dishonesty and for exploiting their own people. On the face of it, Levi's reaction to Jesus is astonishing

---

125 Luke 5:8.
126 Luke 5:27–28.

– immediate, uninhibited and absolute. He had much to leave, but he left it based on the power of one man's call. Over the centuries, thousands of others have done the same, completely reorienting their lives. Have you heard Jesus' clear call to leave something behind? What would you do if you did? He may not, for example, want you to lock your office door and never return, or leave your laboratory, office or study. But he might want you to return there as a completely changed person whose mind has "left everything" that previously preoccupied it and so effectively shut him out.

3. *One thankful leper.* "He threw himself at Jesus' feet and thanked him – and he was a Samaritan."[127] As Jesus travelled in the border country between Samaria and Galilee, ten lepers called to him in a loud voice, "Jesus, Master, have pity on us!"[128] It is very difficult for us to imagine the passion and desperation behind that cry. Lepers were social outcasts – rejects from society. Jesus did have pity on them, and all ten were healed, but only one came back to give him thanks. We have no idea why. The others might have been equally grateful that their lives were restored, that they could return to their families and reintegrate into society. But they never went back to the source of their blessing to give thanks. We need to come to God with thanksgiving, but we can only do that if we acknowledge what he has given us, how he has healed us. These lepers knew exactly what they needed. Perhaps you have been hesitating for a long time about whether you really need Jesus. Notice especially the sequence in this incident: it begins with a recognition of need; followed by a cry for help; then there is a response of healing; and finally a giving of thanks to the healer. We ignore this sequence at our peril, because we can't take shortcuts with

---

[127] Luke 17:16.
[128] Luke 17:13.

God! The nineteenth-century English poet Anne Bronte illustrates the conflict and resolution of the penitent person before God, finally seeing the encouragement of heaven above and beyond the derision and difficulty of the world.

The Penitent

I mourn with thee, and yet rejoice
That thou shouldst sorrow so;
With angel choirs I join my voice
To bless the sinner's woe.

Though friends and kindred turn away,
And laugh they grief to scorn;
I hear the great Redeemer say,
"Blessed are ye that mourn."

Hold on thy course, nor deem it strange
That earthly cords are riven:
Man may lament the wondrous change,
But "there is joy in heaven!"

Reflection:

Thomas à Kempis once said, "I would rather feel remorse than know how to define it." A genuine sense of penitence characterized these three people who met Jesus and responded to him, conscious of their own guilt. How do you react to the penitent and their plight? With pity? Scorn? Detachment? Empathy? Sympathy? Are you penitent? Why or why not?

Reactions to hearing the apostles

Following are the stories of three individuals who heard Paul explain the gospel in the early days of the church. The New Testament book of Acts records their reactions.

1. Lydia. Paul and his team were in Philippi, a major city in Macedonia, and looking for a place to pray on the Sabbath. People at that time encouraged visitors like Paul to explore ideas by speaking in public places. And Paul took every opportunity to do that. Lydia (a dealer in purple cloth from Thyatira) was in the audience, and she emerged as a worshipper of God. While we don't know the details of how this happened in Lydia's heart and mind, we do know that she trusted God and spent time with others of like mind. But the book of Acts records that something else happened to her. "The Lord opened her heart to respond to Paul's message."[129] Paul's message would have explained the life, death and resurrection of Jesus. Lydia either had not heard about Jesus, or had not yet expressed her faith in him. You might identify with Lydia. You might have respect and reverence for God and even meet with other worshippers, but you might not have put your faith in Jesus. Only you can do that. The final book in the Bible, Revelation, gives us this image of Jesus waiting to become a part of our lives: "Here I am! I stand at the door and knock. If anyone hears my voice and opens the door, I will come in and eat with them, and they with me."[130] The last sentence depicts intimacy as friends and family enjoy a relaxed meal in each other's company – this tells us much about the relationship Jesus offers to us.

2. Felix. Paul was on trial before the governor Felix. Felix was well acquainted with the "Way" – the term used to

---

[129] Acts 16:14.
[130] Revelation 3:20.

describe faith in Jesus Christ, since he opened up a new way to God through his death and resurrection. Felix had no shortage of data about the content and impact of Jesus' message as he contemplated what to do with Paul. He postponed a decision and, days later, returned to this contentious case involving Paul, a Roman citizen with a high profile. "As Paul discoursed (with Felix) on righteousness, self-control and the judgment to come, Felix was afraid and said, 'That's enough for now! You may leave. When I find it convenient, I will send for you.'"[131] Felix obviously knew enough about these subjects to be able to discuss them with one of the finest theologians of his generation – yet we have no evidence that he ever became a believer. Nor do we know why he was afraid of becoming one.

I had a devout Jewish colleague some years ago who spent at least two hours every day studying the Torah. I asked him once how God spoke to him through this exercise. He retorted fiercely. "This is nothing to do with hearing from God. For me, it's an intellectual exercise." Perhaps that is all it ever was for Felix, because we never read that it was "convenient" to send for Paul.

3. *Agrippa*. After his interview with Felix, Paul continued to defend his beliefs before King Agrippa. With Agrippa as his audience, Paul chronicled his own career path – from persecuting Christians to his conversion and his heavenly commission to preach the good news of Jesus Christ to the Gentiles.

Agrippa was familiar with these events from his investigation of numerous Jewish allegations about Paul's behaviour. Paul did not merely present facts and figures to the king, however. He spoke with passion and was looking

---

[131] Acts 24:25.

for a result – a dramatic change in Agrippa's life. Agrippa understood this and asked Paul, "Do you think that in such a short time you can persuade me to become a Christian?" Paul replied, "Short time or long – I pray God that not only you but all who are listening to me today may become what I am, except for these chains".[132] Agrippa gave Paul an attentive ear. Because he took the time to listen and understand, he recognized Paul's innocence in the face of these charges. But, as with Felix, there is no evidence that Agrippa ever declared a personal faith in Jesus Christ. Perhaps he did need more time, although none of us ever know how much time we have. I invite you to consider whether this may be your time.

Food for thought:

We have posed and answered three questions in this chapter: Where were you? What happens now? What did they do? The fourth and final question is one that only you can answer: What will you do?

---

[132] Acts 26:28–29.

By the same author:

Whose Life is it Anyway?
(Carlisle: Authentic Lifestyle, 2002).

God's Payroll – Whose Work is it Anyway?
(Carlisle: Authentic Lifestyle, 2003).

God's Wealth – Whose Money is it Anyway?
(Carlisle: Authentic Lifestyle, 2004).

Learning at the Crossroads
(Milton Keynes: Authentic Media, 2005).